Praise for *Even If It Kills Me*

"A rock musician chronicles his adventures at a taekwondo dojo in Texas.

"Blair's debut book is a whirlwind through his broad range of experiences and eclectic interests. He is primarily known as a bassist for the alternative rock band the Toadies, whom readers may know for their 1994 hit 'Possum Kingdom.' But while Blair recounts his escapades with the band on the road throughout the work, the memoir mainly discusses the author's love of martial arts. After settling with his wife in Amarillo, Texas, Blair decided to get in better shape by picking up a passion from his past: taekwondo. He takes the reader on a tour of the limited dojo offerings throughout the city before settling on a World Taekwondo Federation dojang led by a coach for the U.S. Olympic team. Shortly thereafter, Blair was a white belt in his early forties, sparring with teenagers far above his skill level, getting regular lessons in humility. The author writes in a wandering, conversational tone that can be digressive and difficult to follow at times. Occasionally, he includes personal critiques of his younger sparring partners that can seem oddly vindictive, but most of the time the narrative voice is amusing despite the excess of superfluous anecdotes. Once Blair settles into his dojang, he takes the reader through his growing obsession with taekwondo. He acquired equipment, trained constantly, and slowly won the respect and friendship of his more experienced peers in his quest to attain a black belt. Along the way, he learned a clichéd but heartwarming lesson about the philosophical value of martial arts: 'Knowing kicks and punches is not what keeps us protected. It's the values and the self [...] that allow us to live life and be better people.' In addit[ion ...] [...] his account should please readers looking fo[r ...] a strange pocket of American culture [...]

"An uneven but charming[ly ...] [...]ailing a bassist's martial arts journey."

—*Kirkus Reviews*

*   *   *

"*Even If It Kills Me* is an honest, sometimes brutal (and often hilarious) account of author Donivan Blair's endeavors. From watching kung fu movies as a kid to joining an international touring band to ultimately revisiting his 'first obsession' and becoming a black belt in his forties, Mr. Blair takes us along for his wild ride. But even more than an amazing journey, it's also a story about honesty, integrity, and hope. As someone who's pursued both music and fitness, *Even If It Kills Me* resonates on multiple levels.

"Mr. Blair's accurate description of playing in bands ('beg for gigs, play for no one, sleep in a van . . .') will have you laughing out loud, while the chapter on the death of his father will leave you in tears. Still, the anecdote of training alongside real Korean black belts will make you blush as you share his humility.

"One of my favorite passages is when Blair beautifully extolls the virtues of practice—he compares musical notes with the steps of *taegeuk*, making the connection between 'forms' in martial arts and technical exercises on a musical instrument. He states how both 'train your body to get the details right.' I have shared similar sentiments myself, but have never expressed them so clearly. Amazing!

"Ultimately, this book is all about emotion, joy, and pain. No matter where you are in your respective journey in life, *Even If It Kills Me* is full of valuable lessons and wildly entertaining stories. Highly recommended."

—Danny Kavadlo, world-renowned fitness trainer and
#1 best-selling author of *Strength Rules*

*   *   *

"There's no way for me to not be biased here. The author is my brother, and unlike most siblings, we actually get along, love each other, and genuinely enjoy each other's time. We talk every day. He's my 'true north,' I suppose you could say. All that having been said, this is a great book, and I think it can appeal to anyone. Not just musicians and not just martial artists, but anyone that has tried to beat seemingly insurmountable odds, anyone that's been told they can't, and anyone that believes in themselves when all hope seems lost. This book is for the little guys in the small towns and the average people. This book is for self-believers. This book is for fighters."

—Zachariah Blair, lead guitarist, Rise Against

*   *   *

"Not only did Donivan Blair make his mark on the world of punk, rock, alternative rock, pop-punk, and sundry other subsects of messing up your hearing with bands such as Hagfish and the Toadies, but for Donivan to get his black belt at age forty-three just sums up the never-surrender ethos that makes guys like this lifers."

—Mike Gitter, vice president of A&R,
Century Media Records

EVEN IF IT KILLS ME

MARTIAL ARTS, ROCK AND ROLL, AND MORTALITY

Donivan Blair
with T. G. LaFredo

YMAA Publication Center
Wolfeboro, NH USA

YMAA Publication Center, Inc.
  PO Box 480
  Wolfeboro, New Hampshire 03894
  1-800-669-8892 • info@ymaa.com • www.ymaa.com

ISBN: 9781594395390 (print) • ISBN: 9781594395406 (ebook)

Publisher's Cataloging in Publication

Names: Blair, Donivan, author. | LaFredo, T. G., author.
Title: Even if it kills me : martial arts, rock and roll, and mortality / Donivan Blair with T. G. LaFredo.
Description: Wolfeboro, NH USA : YMAA Publication Center, [2017]
Identifiers: ISBN: 9781594395390 (print) | 9781594395406 (ebook) | LCCN: 2017951961
Subjects: LCSH: Blair, Donivan. | Tae kwon do--Training. | Martial arts--Training. | Martial artists--
              Biography. | Rock musicians--United States--Biography. | Toadies (Musical group) |
              LCGFT: Autobiographies. | BISAC: SPORTS & RECREATION / Martial Arts & Self-Defense. |
              BIOGRAPHY & AUTOBIOGRAPHY / General. | BIOGRAPHY & AUTOBIOGRAPHY /
              Artists, Architects, Photographers.

Classification: LCC: GV1113.B53 B53 2017 | DDC: 796.8/092 --dc23

TABLE OF CONTENTS

PREFACE: GOING BACK

I WALKED AWAY.

That's what I've felt for all these years.

As a kid, martial arts were my first love, my first real obsession. My brother Zach and I wanted to be ninjas when we grew up. We watched old kung fu movies and pounded on each other. Zach shot me in the ear with an arrow. On separate occasions he hit me in the head with a bat and *nunchaku*—not "numb chucks," goddamn it. I got in my licks too.

Later we took up taekwondo. It's not like there was a ninja school in Sherman, Texas. We loved it though. We could beat the shit out of other kids instead of one another. But our family didn't have much money, and classes became expensive. In time we bowed out. We gave up on being ninjas and took part in real life.

Well, sort of real life. We pursued punk rock.

We first found our way in Hagfish, a band my brother and I started in Sherman. We made a few records, traveled the world, and learned about the business. Today Zach plays guitar in Rise Against. Since 2008 I've been with the Toadies. I'm not a rock star. I play bass. Tens of people know me.

At this point you may be saying, "I bought a book by a bass player?" Or even, "Bass players can read?" I know. It's pretty surprising.

After years of making records and playing shows, the Toadies have decided to take some time off. I've gone home to Amarillo. I'm finally going to be in one place for a while, which gives me the opportunity to return to taekwondo. It's always bothered me that I left before really getting good—way before attaining those mystical powers that come with the vaunted black belt.

That is reason enough to do this, but something else is also on my mind. Something about simplifying. I want to return to the days before my life revolved around four strings and arguing with three people about a flat 7. I want to return to a time when I felt free of obligations and I had real, honest hope in my heart. I was a kid, my dad was still alive, and my only real concern was what comic book I should read next.

I'm not a kid anymore. I'm a middle-aged man trying to come to grips with being a middle-aged man. I'm not as fast as I used to be. It takes longer for the injuries to heal. I have to eat more bran.

But if I don't do this now, when will I? Never. That's when.

I am a forty-year-old white belt. I'm going back.

FIRST CLASS

S HERMAN, TEXAS, 1982. Every kid's heroes were the Von Erichs, Rambo, and Ronnie Reagan. Don't like it? You're a girl.

In the Blair household we were all about the ninjas. My brother Zach and I watched weekly ninja matinées on channel 39 from Dallas. All the characters wore black belts, so to us it seemed every badass had one. A black belt is not the real reason you should study martial arts, but try telling that to a little kid. I imagined a secret black-belt club with shadowy initiations, passwords, and rituals. Actually, I still imagine it that way. Even as a ten-year-old I knew getting a black belt would be an effort that might kill me—which made it that much more attractive. I wanted in.

A new school, Rick's Taekwondo, had just opened in town. All of my friends were going, and Zach and I wanted to join them. It would have cost fifty dollars per month for us to go, and my parents just couldn't afford it. They had both lost their jobs, and times were tough in our house.

Mamaw, my grandmother Naomi, had the solution. She worked at Texas Instruments, which had a health club for employees and their families. One of the men she worked with, Calvin Anoatubby, had begun teaching taekwondo there. Master Calvin was a full-blooded Cherokee and a former student of Demetrius "Golden Greek" Havanas, who won the grand nationals in 1974. The guys were legit. We just had to get into those classes.

With Mamaw's employee discount, maybe my parents could afford to send us. We'd give it a try. Mamaw got us enrolled. I was ten, and Zach was nine. We were finally on our way to ninjahood.

We went to the health club for our first class. Kids and parents filed in a few at a time. The *dojang*, or taekwondo school, had low, flat ceilings; mirrors on one side; assorted exercise equipment; and a mat that covered the floor. It was like any other martial arts studio I would ever see, except ours smelled of chlorine from the Jacuzzi next door.

We had no idea what to expect—or what was expected of us. Before Master Calvin had a chance to call the class to attention, my brother and I decided to impress everyone with a little demonstration of our ninja moves. Zach did flips, or tried anyway, and threw imaginary Chinese stars. I threw smoke bombs—also imaginary—and disappeared with a *whoosh*, cartwheeling away.

We both had attention deficit disorder. I repeat, both of us. And no, my parents didn't get much sleep. This demonstration was just a sample of what they put up with at home.

After our "audition" Master Calvin called the class to order. He instructed us on how and when to bow. Before you get on the mat, you have to bow. Before you leave the mat, you have to bow. If you have to run off the mat for a piece of equipment or take a pee and come back, you bow off and then bow back on. All this bowing shows respect for your teacher. It also suggests why so many martial artists have back problems.

Next Master Calvin led us in stretches. The first one was the butterfly. You place the bottoms of your feet together and bounce your knees up and down, stretching your thigh and calf muscles. Zach really exerted himself. He farted. It was loud. He would do this at least once a week for the duration of our TKD studies. Did he and I laugh? Every single time.

Then we learned the proper way to throw a straight punch. It looked a little different from the way Bruce Lee did it, but oh well. Maybe you could still "make it unto a thing of iron."

We couldn't help but notice how good the other students were. Their kicks had snap and, unlike ours, didn't look like overcooked asparagus when thrown. Punches were synchronized and accompanied with loud "hiyahs!" at the right time. They could jump and spin-kick on cue. We couldn't do any of that. I think that was when it dawned on us that maybe we didn't have awesome skills—or any skills at all.

The other kids were not only good but sharp and bright in their white *doboks*, martial arts uniforms. They wore colored belts too—yellow, green, red, and blue—and looked way cooler than we did in our hand-me-down cutoff shorts and thrift-store shirts.

After class Master Calvin said in order to continue we would have to attend in doboks of our own. He knew our family couldn't really afford them, and he handled the situation with dignity, allowing us a few weeks to come up with something. My parents could barely afford the classes, even with Mamaw's discount. When we told my dad we would need uniforms, he didn't take it too well. How were they going to afford more clothes? We barely had enough money for the Kmart crap we already wore.

Mamaw came to the rescue again. She had sewn vampire capes, cowboy costumes, and Zorro masks, so plain doboks were a cinch. Mamaw was a wiz with the Singer. She asked what color we wanted. Black, of course—like a ninja's.

Our new doboks were amazing. We were so proud of them. We wore them to class—and to bed. I would have worn mine to school except I didn't need extra incentive for students to make fun of

The Blair kids. We came. We saw. We
kicked ass.

me. I felt like Kane Kosugi in *Revenge of the Ninja*. You know,
except he was Japanese and talented. I was Texan and not.

Despite Mamaw's discount, TKD classes were expensive for my
parents. Even at ten years old I knew that. As much as I wanted
to be Danny Rand, I still felt awful and guilty about the cost.

At some point my mom got a new job, so she had a little more
money, and she kept finding a way to come up with the monthly
fees. My parents made sure to get us to the health club three nights
a week. If they were paying, we were going. We never missed a
class, and we practiced every night at home.

Taekwondo was all I thought about. At night TKD took me
off to dreamland. I did cartwheels and somersaults through the
air, kicking ass while dressed in ninja black. When I was pent up
at school, I thought of taekwondo. If I had a fight with my brother,
which was most of the time, taekwondo helped. Instead of taking
wild potshots at each other like before, now our fighting was struc-
tured. The only problem was that when I kicked my brother in
the nose, I could no longer say it was an accident.

Zach and I actually started to get good, and all that exercise
calmed us down, something my parents previously thought

impossible. All along my mom had refused to put us on Ritalin, even though everyone, including my dad, begged her to. Martial arts were a perfect solution. They pretty much kept our ADD in check.

Granted, before every class, Zach still ran into the sauna next door, thinking he might see women in their bikinis. He always got in trouble for it, though that never dissuaded him. Still, we were doing much better overall.

In five months we advanced from white belt to yellow to green. Master Calvin said that was fast. He told my dad we were the best kickers in class.

The best kickers in class. I carried that compliment everywhere I went.

Soon Master Calvin told us we were ready to test for our blue belts. That was exciting. We were practicing hard and making progress, and our instructor saw it. It was the first time I'd really devoted myself to anything, the first time I saw that hard work makes a difference.

But then my mom lost her job, and we had to quit taekwondo. Zach and I wanted to go back, but eventually we gave up on the idea. No sense in putting more pressure on my parents. They gave us what we needed; they just couldn't afford what we wanted.

SEARCHING FOR A SCHOOL

I F THIS were a movie, we'd put a line of text across the bottom of the screen: THIRTY YEARS LATER.

Thirty years? A lot happened in that time, but this is mainly a martial arts story, and in that respect, not a lot happened for me. Zach and I were busy playing music, first together and later in separate bands. We did make it out of Sherman.

Dallas was my home base for ten years. In 2001 my wife, Shelley, got a job offer 360 miles north, in the Texas Panhandle. That brought us to Amarillo. The Yellow City. The Yellow Rose of Texas. The world capital of cow shit.

I admit, when we got here, I was really disappointed with where life had taken me. I missed my brother and my friends. I missed having great musicians to work with. Amarillo culture—if you can use those two words together—didn't make it any easier.

Like most of Tejas, Amarillo is as conservative as you get. People in DFW and Austin are fairly open minded, but in Amarillo,

Lubbock, or Sherman? No way. What would these people say if they knew I voted for Obama—twice?

And can you believe people here go to church? On purpose? That was a new one for me.

The Panhandle is a bastion of ultraconservative, über-religious thought—and I know those words don't go together. Amarillo has more churches per capita than any other city in the state. We used to have a twenty-four-hour truck stop called the Jesus Christ Is Lord Travel Center. In the town of Groom, forty miles from here, you can visit the Cross of Our Lord Jesus Christ. It's a nineteen-story cross—2.5 million pounds of steel, visible from twenty miles away. It's probably visible from space. The Prince of Peace is all about exclamation points.

But wait! There's more! While you're there, you can visit the life-size Stations of the Cross and the tomb of our Savior. Because, you know, Jesus died and rose again—in Texas.

I've visited the megacross. I've also visited Sexmuseum Amsterdam Venustempel. I went to that one twice.

But enough with the politics and religion. That stuff never ends in Amarillo, but it will end in this book. It's no way to treat a reader. Let's just say for a long time I wondered what I did wrong to end up here. I became depressed and ate too much, and soon I had put on thirty pounds. Not only did I feel like shit, but I looked like shit too.

Eventually I met up with Barry, a good guy who had trained in martial arts since his teens. We struck up a friendship based on our mutual love for kung fu movies. We got together once in a while to watch Bruce Lee flicks or *The 36th Chamber of Shaolin* or *Iron Monkey*.

Barry said someday he wanted to start his own martial arts school, and he asked if I'd like to train with him. I thought I'd give it a shot. We got together three times a week. We worked out in his garage, practicing karate kicks, punches, and blocks.

Barry lived and breathed this stuff. His energy and enthusiasm were contagious. I was having fun, and in a few months I had lost all that weight. My skills were improving, and my love for the martial arts came back with a vengeance.

When I was a kid, I dreamed of the magical powers I'd possess by the time I earned my black belt. Even at forty, my image of this pursuit wasn't that much different. I envisioned myself progressing through the ranks, but that posed a bit of a problem when it came to training with Barry. The guy knew his stuff and really studied hard, but he was largely self-taught. I felt I needed to train at a formal school with a clear lineage.

In other words, I wanted a black belt.

I know: an actual black belt would look down on me for that. But don't we all have goals? Aren't we all after attainment?

I parted ways with my friend and decided to search for another school. I'll never forget him and all he did to reinvigorate my passion for martial arts.

Now, about that school.

I did some research and began calling around. Amarillo had a varied community of martial artists and styles. I tried all of them.

Kenpo. The instructor reminded me of a cross between Link Wray and Phil Spector. Not a good combination. He was jaded, arrogant, and only in it to pay the bills—the kind of guy who teaches because he doesn't know what else to do and he's too scared to try something new. I met a lot of people like that, sorry to say.

Link Spector called most of the techniques "kill strokes." Pretty cheesy. I stuck around long enough to pass my yellow-sash test, but I felt empty afterward, like I didn't deserve it. And I didn't. I wouldn't have passed me. But he wanted to keep me there and figured I would leave if I didn't advance in rank.

I took a trip out of town, and I was thinking when I got back, I'd tell my teacher I needed to try something else. We never had that conversation. Shelley called and said she saw him on TV.

"Cool," I said. "Did he get an award from the community?"

"No," she said. "He was arrested for child porn."

Krav maga. Then there was the guy who advertised that he was an official krav maga instructor. Krav maga was created by Imi Lichtenfeld, an Israeli martial artist. His mission was to design a system that was easy to understand and apply with little training time. It's famously nasty. I had researched it and decided to give this teacher a call.

On the phone he told me krav maga was created by the Jews. "And since Jews have all the money in the world," he said, "they can afford to hire masters from every art to make krav better." The guy said he'd studied every form of martial art and decided to fuse his knowledge into his own style.

I thanked him and hung up.

Karate. I tried Shotokan and goju-ryu. I liked both styles—and both instructors, actually—but the positions felt too static. I still wanted something more.

I realized I'd been gauging all other styles against the taekwondo I learned as a kid. Maybe TKD was the answer. I've always had to finish what I started, be it a two-mile run, a chocolate cake, or the entire *Conan the Barbarian* series in paperback. That's OCD in action, y'all.

I checked out a TKD school not far from my house. The place was expensive, but I signed up. My fees were supposed to include a uniform, but no one ever came up with one for me. No one introduced me to the instructors or students. Not a single person attempted to show me . . . anything.

In class we would form two lines, face one another, and go through some goofy drills. I was only a white belt, but it seemed I was better than any of the upper-level students. That doesn't mean I'm well skilled; these people just sucked.

The search continued. Maybe I'd left Barry too soon.

THE LOCAL WTF AFFILIATE

I was sitting in my car, staring at the front door of the dojang, too scared to go in and too scared to leave. A couple of kids ran past, shouting, happy to be somewhere other than school or home. I recognized that excitement. I was one of those kids a long time ago. One night I bowed to Master Calvin and left the dojang. Somehow thirty years had passed.

There I was in a parking lot in Amarillo, at my local affiliate of the World Taekwondo Federation. My stomach was rumbling from nerves. It always does when I put myself in an unfamiliar situation like going into a strange school and possibly putting my hands—my moneymakers—at risk. In those instances I think of that line from *The Big Lebowski*: "Donny, you're out of your element."

A week earlier I had set up that first meeting. I called and spoke to the grandmaster, who gave me the OK to attend a free class. At least I think I got the OK. It was kind of hard to understand him over the phone. But there I was outside the dojang, and it was go time.

"Well," I told myself, "you're an idiot for doing this. But you're a loser if you don't at least try."

I got out of my car, took a deep breath, and walked to the door. I was starting on a new path, and I had no idea where it would lead, which was terrifying and exhilarating. The old me—the one who had settled into a comfortable routine—would have backed away, returned to my car, and split. This new guy was at least trying something. Maybe I'd be OK.

One of the senior students, Lois, greeted me at the front desk with a smile and forms to sign. They were the typical waivers that said, essentially, "If you break your neck, it's not our fault." All martial arts schools use them. If you ever go to a place that does not make you sign one, run like hell. They probably have no idea what they're doing, and someone's going to get killed.

The grandmaster's studio, on the other hand, was safe. I'd probably only get maimed.

I signed away life and limb, and the grandmaster walked out from his office to introduce himself. My hand was clammy. His was not. I was auditioning his school, so to speak, but he wasn't trying to impress me.

In my search for a dojang I had learned that the grandmaster was the head of the Texas branch of the World Taekwondo Federation. He was a coach for the US Olympic taekwondo team and had promoted hundreds of people to black belt in his thirty-plus years of teaching.

He had a warm, infectious smile and wore a pristine white dobok. His belt was flawless, the ends hanging in exact symmetry. This is regulation, especially for black belts. You need a sharp uniform and a perfect belt, or you get a sharp, perfect reprimand.

The grandmaster led me on a tour of his school. The main room had a spring-activated floor with mirrors on one wall. The opposite wall had posters depicting all eight *taegeuk*, the forms all taekwondo students must memorize.

Each end was covered with benches for visiting parents to watch while oohhing and ahhing over their children's clumsy attempts at kicking and form work. One area was devoted to boards, wooden and foam swords, and staffs.

Fifteen kicking dummies stood in the adjacent room. If those things could talk, they would beg you to end their suffering. Nothing and no one has ever sinned so much as to merit an endless beating from over-sugared ten-year-olds. The floor was covered with a hard blue mat. Like the dummies, it was unforgiving and would give me more sprained toes than actual satisfaction at my performance.

As we toured the place, the grandmaster introduced me to the other students, mostly yellow belts and green belts. I felt goofy and vulnerable, and I began to wonder if they were judging me. Did they see me as the weird old guy? Were they sizing me up to punch me? This is a by-product of my teenage years. My school was full of bullies and assholes, so even at forty, I distrusted new people.

The grandmaster introduced me to Conner Simpson, the main instructor. Conner was less than a year away from testing for his fourth-degree black belt. That would make him *Master Simpson*—all at the age of twenty-two. I wasn't jealous or anything.

Conner was a nice guy too, but I think he wanted to make an impression. He was leading my free class, and he intended to make me feel it in the morning. I'm sure he thought, "Let's see what the old guy can do."

Maybe that wasn't it. Maybe I was just self-conscious about starting over at nearly twice Conner's age.

We started class with a warm-up, and by "warm-up" I mean we ran twenty laps around the training hall. I kept up with everyone, which seemed to impress the other students. It sure as hell impressed me. It's not like I was some out-of-shape desk jockey. I can run, but I don't like to unless I'm holding a TV set.

During the course of the evening Conner instructed us in kicking and blocking techniques. It started coming back to me. The workout was hot and difficult. At one point I thought about slipping out the back door. I made it through the night, though, and apparently I held my own because before I left, the grand-master invited me back.

Hell yes, I was going back. After all that time away, I would be a martial artist again. I was a stud. A badass.

Then the badass went home and crawled into a hot bath. The adrenaline had worn off, and everything hurt. Everything. That night I cried myself to sleep and prayed for death.

Unfortunately, I awoke the next morning. Through my early morning haze I heard the sounds of mewling and whining. I discovered I was the one doing said mewling and whining. But all I could think of was going back to class.

TRAINING NIGHTS

I'M WORKING out seven times a week now. I train at the dojang Tuesday, Thursday, and Saturday, and I train at home Monday, Wednesday, Friday, and Saturday. I made Saturday a double session, so on Sunday I rest and hang out with the wife. She's encouraged me in all of this, even though she figured it would take over my life. It has, but she's still cool with it.

Like many martial arts, as you learn taekwondo, you progress through different colored belts. The rank structure at the grandmaster's school goes like this: white, orange, yellow, green stripe, green, blue stripe, blue, red stripe, red, black stripe, and then black, which is, of course, when you receive those aforementioned mystical powers.

I am one of eight people in the adult class. Here's the roster:

- Spencer, age fifty, black belt. Spencer is an accountant. He first took up taekwondo to have something to do with his daughter. She reached blue belt and didn't care anymore, but he decided to keep going. The guy works his ass off. He never leaves class dry.

- Sam, seventeen, second-degree black belt. Sam is home-schooled for religious reasons, so he's very, very insulated from the world. The kid has an inner fire that is impressive—and pretty scary. It could either lead to great things or get him on TV for killing his family in their sleep. A hefty dose of religion will do that to you. Sam never—and I do mean *never*—washes his dobok. During sparring sessions the smell alone can win him matches.

- Lee, sixteen, black belt. Lee is half Hispanic and half Chinese, and he gets picked on a lot at school. He's an angry kid because of it. He tells us about the fights he gets into, but I've never seen a scratch on him. I guess his training is paying off. Lee is the fastest and most accurate kicker in class. He's crazy good, but he can't stand being hit hard. It makes him go berserker. And because I can't get the asshole big-brother syndrome out of my head, I like to hit him hard to see what happens. I can't help it.

- Eric, fifteen, already a second-degree black belt. Eric reached that rank younger than most, so he was of the opinion that he knew everything, and he was happy to tell you so. At first he got on my nerves, but I've changed my mind about him. He does know a lot and has great focus, dedication, and skill. The kid has gained my respect, even though I'm older than his father.

  If anyone in our group has the capacity to become a great teacher, it is Eric. The grandmaster sees this and is making an instructor of him. That has created some animosity between Sam and Eric. Being seventeen, Sam doesn't want to take instruction from a fifteen-year-old.

- Conner, twenty-six, third-degree black belt. Conner is a great guy and my first instructor. He taught me all the fundamentals. He and Lois run the school for the grandmaster.

- Joe, around twenty-five, fifth-degree black belt. Joe is the grandmaster's son. The entire organization is his if he wants it. The guy's talent is uncanny, but I don't know if he cares. Maybe if you do something your entire life and you're great at it, it means less to you. If I had half of his ability, I could actually sleep at night.

    I take that back. I wouldn't sleep. I'd be too busy flipping insane tornado kicks at will, just because I could.

- Owen, sixteen, red belt. Owen is a high-functioning autistic kid. He's really angry, which must be due in part to being gay in Amarillo.

    Gay in Amarillo: now there's a book for you.

    The kid has just come out of the closet. I feel for him because he's determined and because he has a lot to deal with, but then he opens his mouth and ruins it. He's arrogant and an all-around pain in the ass.

    Here's my honest assessment of his skills. His cardio is shit. His blocks are horrible. He couldn't punch his way out of a takeout box. He wouldn't beat a ten-year-old girl in a push-up contest. But holy shit can he kick. It's ridiculous. How can he be so deficient in so many ways but kick like a motherfucker? This kid could kick his way through a wall, yell "Oh yeah" like the Kool-Aid Man, and then drop a gorilla with a roundhouse.

- Finally, there's Donivan, the forty-year-old white belt. Bass player. Strengths include motivation, flexibility, and the ability to buy beer. That's about it.

When I trained with Barry, I tried a lot of strikes and techniques, but I never found one that made me worry about my bones or ligaments—or mental capacity, for that matter. Taekwondo is different. I think the grandmaster is trying to kill us.

A typical class goes like this. We run ten laps one way, then ten in the opposite direction. I feel like I'm going to die of cardiac arrest. It's easy for my classmates, and they rub it in my face. I've said how I feel about running, so I won't dwell on it, but it is at least a good warm-up before the stretching exercises that make this old body feel like Silly Putty.

I am getting farther in my stretches and gaining confidence, but, honestly, I've been pretty flexible my entire life. When I was training with Barry, I'd try front kicks and axe kicks, and he'd say, "I wish I was as limber as you." I hadn't thought it was anything special. I just put my leg straight up in the air.

Next there's a strict punching sequence. Koreans love order. We punch ten times but only when the instructor gives the command, which is usually yelled in Korean. Then we double-punch another ten times. The punches felt weird to me at first. With Barry I learned to cock my fist high up on the abdomen. In taekwondo we cock them lower, just above the waist. In the first few classes I struggled to make the adjustment, but once I did, wow, what a difference: I looked like a forty-year-old guy who had just relearned to punch.

On kicking nights we kick up and down the length of the dojang. We go from easiest to most difficult: front, roundhouse, side, back, jumping front, axe, and tornado. Each side. As a lower belt I haven't learned all of the kicks yet. I watch the upper belts perform axe and tornado, and I feel a bit jealous that I can't join them.

That's just the end of the warm-up. By then I'm dripping wet and ready to go home, but it's time to hit the bags.

We go to the next room, which has three hanging bags and about fifteen Wavemaster kicking bags. We start the kicking sequence again, attacking each of the bags and working our way down the length of the room. When we get back to our starting point, we go through once more, kicking with the opposite leg. Each. Goddamn. Kick.

Then the grandmaster yells, "Combinations!" and it all starts over. I buy a lot of fucking Epsom salt on kicking nights.

If we can breathe and we're still upright after all of that, we move on to taegeuk.

Some martial artists bitch about forms. This is especially true for MMA guys. A lot of them say forms are flowery and a waste of time. They compare them to dances and say, "What, if someone attacks you, are you going to step back and perform this whole sequence?" That argument has led some modern schools to abandon forms altogether.

I think those people have missed the point.

Forms are my favorite part of the night. They allow me to take my time, focus, and concentrate on each step. The goal is perfection, and it's easy to see the parallel with technical exercises on a musical instrument. You play scales, arpeggios, and *études* over and over again. It's not a race, just as taegeuk practice is not a death match. Both are meditative. Both train your body to get the details right.

Those notes are the building blocks of a song. Those steps are the building blocks of a taegeuk. Done correctly, it is a thing of beauty, an outlet for an accomplished martial artist to convey power, strength, speed, and confidence.

In my case they look like the dance Elaine used to do on *Seinfeld*.

After taegeuk, it's almost time to bow out and call it a night. But first, push-ups. Why? Because we aren't dead yet, and the grandmaster wants to give it one more shot.

When we finally finish, I can't wait to bow out, go home, and soak. Then I go to bed, turn out the light, and hope I won't die in my sleep.

That's the average night at the dojang, but on Thursday, we endure a different kind of suffering. We spar.

I don't like to spar unless it's with someone around my age—which limits the choices. The older guys look out for each other and keep some sense of self-preservation. We get to test our skills, but neither guy wants to hurt the other because, unlike most of the walking zit factories with belts around their waists, we've actually been in fights. We understand the reality of violence, and that reality is that it sucks. Sometimes it finds you and you have to do something about it. But it does suck.

None of this means anything to amped-up testosterone-fueled teenage boys. For them it's *kill, kill, kill.* I get it. It's a tough age. They want to be cool, but Mom and Dad are still dropping them off everywhere. They want to have hair on their chests—or maybe they don't; I don't know what kids are into. They want to get laid, but they're afraid to talk to girls . . . and Mom and Dad are still dropping them off everywhere.

All that frustration adds up, and these kids are pretty much ready to burst. They have the strong desire to punish someone, anyone. Drive them hard and they lose their cool—oh wait, they don't have that.

It's a mismatch for the old guys. We all get laid, own cars, and have hairy chests, so what's there to prove?

SOMEWHERE ELSE

When you're a kid, you dream big dreams. I used to have all these
fantasies about superheroes, and a rock and roll musician, in a way,
was a tangible embodiment of a superhero. I wasn't going to be
Superman. I couldn't leap tall buildings. But I could make music.
—Geddy Lee[1]
Bassist and lead vocalist, Rush

I AM a lifelong comic geek, and by the time I hit high school, I
was a full-on band geek. I spent my days and nights obsessing
about Rush, the Police, Iron Maiden, the Misfits, Anthrax, King's
X, Celtic Frost, Voivod, Yngwie Malmsteen . . . the list goes on.

I'd also gotten way into horror, science fiction, and fantasy
books. But when I say fantasy, I mean Conan, none of the
Fellowship "We are friends for life" bullshit. Robert E. Howard's
hero got ripped, slew monsters, and screwed girls with huge

---

1. *Rock Icons.* "Geddy Lee: The Maestro." Episode 101. Ralph Chapman, Sam Dunn.
VH1, February 21, 2015.

knockers on a daily basis. Once you've read that stuff, the typical guy-on-a-quest story is kind of lame. I could stick a paperback in my blue jean jacket and always have one to escape into. During lunch break, when other kids would smoke outside, I'd wolf down my food and head to the library to read Lovecraft. No wonder I never got laid.

Music, comics, speculative fiction—one thing they have in common is they all transport you somewhere else. As a kid, that's where I wanted to be: anywhere other than Sherman, Texas.

Being a teenager is awkward no matter who you are. Maybe the cool kids just conceal it better. I was not a cool kid. I preferred imaginative worlds. They might have violated the laws of time and space, but somehow they still made more sense than Sherman.

My brother Zach and I escaped into music. He took up guitar, and I took up bass. We wanted to put together a killer band. We tried several times in acts such as Lunacy, Forbidden Cause, and Harmzway—with a z. We knew that was our only way out of there. It sure as hell wasn't going to be academia or sports.

We spent every day practicing, either on our own or in band rehearsals. If we were going to get anywhere, we had to hustle. We played before school, after school, and sometimes during school. During lunch hour we rushed home in my canary-yellow Camaro, got in as much playing as we could, and then flew back in time for class. I got a flurry of speeding tickets, but at least I knew how to play "Orion" by Metallica.

In the afternoon we knocked out our homework and spent the rest of the day practicing. We played all weekend. Friends called and said, "Let's go party." We practiced instead.

I still hate parties. A social bee I am not.

It's tough to make a living in music. You work and sacrifice and starve, and there's still no guarantee you'll get anywhere. But the thought of being anything other than musicians never crossed our minds. It seemed to us that we had just two choices: face the uncertainty or waste our lives in Sherman.

Go Bearcats. Do or die.

My seventeen-year-old self would say, "Die, preferably."

Pop quiz: Why does Sherman suck so much?

A. The population of lunkheads who say, "The best things in life are high school football and church, hoss."
B. The backwoods mentality that requires you to fire your Remington 870 straight up in the air on New Year's, Christmas, your birthday, and anytime the Cowboys win.
C. The smell of mayo emanating from the Kraft plant, bumming out people from Denison to Pottsboro.
D. The Oklahoma border. It's just eight miles away, and nothing good can come of that.
E. All of the above.

If you said E, you nailed it. This quiz has been brought to you by the Sherman Council of Travel, Tourism, and Mayonnaise.

Sidenote: I'm slamming Sherman while writing in Amarillo, and if you know about Texas, you'll see the irony in that. I know. Amarillo is not a cultural mecca, but even at its worst, I've always thought, "Hey, at least it's not Sherman."

Eventually, Zach and I made our escape—down Highway 75 to Dallas. It was only forty-five minutes away, but it too was a different world.

Twenty-something years later, we both can say we made a bunch of records and toured the world. Sounds like fun, right? It is. But there's more to it—so much more that it's hard to know where to begin.

Consider this: I have a number of friends who play music part time and live normal lives. Quite a few of them have expressed a desire to quit their day jobs, buy a van, and go on tour. These are

Onstage with Zach. There's more to it than what you see here. (Photo by Karlo X. Ramos)

guys in their forties, mind you, guys with homes and families. They are already successful in their chosen careers, yet they also want to be *somewhere else*. They want to drop all they have to live in a van with three or four other dudes.

No mention of making a record, securing distribution, or getting a booking agent. No mention of PR and marketing. No real thought about gear, logistics, and insurance. Just go on tour and live the life. It's a fantasy, and as long as no one acts on it, no one gets hurt.

To live the life, you will have to . . .

1. beg for gigs
2. play for no one—and I do mean no one
3. sleep in the van you just bought because you have no money because you have played to no one
4. make a daily decision on whether to eat a hot dog—because they are cheap—or splurge on a McDonald's value meal because it will fill you up all day

5. hope to God there is someone in the crowd who will let you sleep on his floor because the van you bought stinks like feet and farts
6. feel satisfied to make it home with fifty bucks
7. hand your wife that fifty bucks and say, "It was a good tour."

I have to ask my friends, "You actually *want* this? Why?"

I want to know if they will teach me how to do their jobs. Then we can switch places, and I won't have to worry about paying my fucking bills a year from now. Because even when you've "made it"—whatever that means—you realize you still have to hustle.

Yes, I graduated from vans to buses, from bars to clubs and arenas, but that took twenty-five years. Everything I have is because I did all that shit work—and a lot more.

I don't mean for any of this to sound self-congratulatory. I am no virtuoso. I just worked hard and took my chances. I knew trying and failing would still be better than sitting at City Limits, nursing a Lone Star beer, reminiscing about that time I caught the winning touchdown pass.

Might as well pull up a stool. You'll be here for the next several decades.

I think about my Quixotic pals who want to quit their real lives and become troubadours. They're kidding themselves. They would be on a collision course with failure. They're outsiders who want in.

But wait. Where martial arts are concerned, I am an outsider who wants in. How deep do the parallels go?

Am I playing at something I know nothing about? Something I could only be good at if I had been at it twenty-five years? Would a veteran martial artist look at me and roll his eyes? Would he say I'm pretending? Maybe he'd think about the broken toes, the bad wrist, and the trick knee and say, "Don't do it. Turn back while you can. Take up knitting instead."

If I'm honest about it, yeah, this is entirely possible. But I will train today, as I did yesterday, as I will tomorrow. I'll approach martial arts as I have music because that's the only way I know.

If a fifteen-year-old kid asked me for some insight into a life in music, this is what I would say: talent is overrated.

You read that right. Make a bass-player joke if you want, but I say talent, schmalent. It all comes down to hard work and making the best use of your time. Anyone can learn to play an instrument. Especially a bass. There are a few prodigies in the world; for the rest of us, it's all about dedication.

I'm counting on that to translate to taekwondo as well. I'm not talented. I'm not a natural athlete. I don't have incredible grace or strength or balance.

I'm just stubborn. I'm just here to go until I can't go any longer.

THE DAO OF ARMADILLO EGGS

T HE MAJORITY of men suffer an identity crisis as they approach middle age. Here's how it goes. You wake up one morning, stumble toward the shower, and catch a glimpse of an awful, misshapen, potbellied mutant peering in the window.

Holy shit. That's not a window. That's the mirror.

Holy shit. That's me.

Turns out that steady diet of fried food, Cokes, and hot dogs has let you down. But the indignity does not end there. You can't read anything without your glasses. You've got hair sprouting everywhere but your cranium. Twenty-one-year-olds look twelve to you, and no matter what you say, you can't dissuade them from calling you sir.

That's OK. Their music sucks anyway.

You're fat now. You're slowing down, and it's obvious in the way you walk and talk and think. You're always reciting the same old anecdotes. Your friends laugh out of politeness, but when you're not around, they say, "Does he not realize he tells the same three stories all the fucking time?"

Best of all, you've lost your sex drive. Maybe it sneaked away during one of those afternoon naps. How would you be able to tell anyway? Your equipment doesn't function as well as it used to.

To stave off the advancing depression, you will do one of three things:

1. Buy a convertible.
2. Buy a hairpiece. *Alternate choice:* Dye the hair you have left. Whichever makes you look more awesomer cruising around with the top down.
3. Buy a new girlfriend. She runs. She jumps. She's oh so flexible. She digs the convertible. And even though she's twenty years your junior, she's totally into your personality. You're funny.

Well, I can't afford a convertible.

I could afford a hairpiece, I guess, but I've been bald since the age of twenty-three, and there's a lot of evidence to prove it. What would people say if one day I just showed up with Fabio's locks?

The girlfriend thing is out too. I've been married more than twenty years, and I am that misshapen mutant, so my wife got the shit end of that stick.

A fourth option, one not nearly as popular as the others, is to get in shape and face whatever the second half of your life may bring. Call it "manning up" if you like.

The American diet makes this much more difficult. If you travel, if you go to restaurants, if you get invited to friends' houses for dinner, chances are that the people around you will be eating a lot of bad stuff, and they will expect you to eat a lot of it too. If this is a family tradition, the habit will be that much harder to break. It doesn't help when you're in Texas, where everything is Texas sized.

When my dad was a kid, he could have blown away in a strong wind. At some point he turned into a two-hundred-fifty-pound monster who could send you to Valhalla with one punch.

What happened? My mom thinks it was her cooking. Makes sense. The woman does not have a light menu. Her meals were quick, cheap, and dense. She had to feed two teenage boys and a golem for a husband.

Once I left the house, my eating habits continued, with the minor hindrance that I had no money. A good day meant having enough to eat at Cicis buffet. I'd go around two or three in the afternoon. That way I could have lunch and dinner at the same time. I'd leave there with a gut full of cheese and dough, and I'd feel stuffed until the next morning.

Then I met Shelley. She was a farm girl, and my God, her meals were amazing. They still are. That's just part of our culture. As they say in Perryton, "What do you call a farm girl who can't cook? A cat owner."

We had been dating for about five months when she first made a meal for me. Usually we'd go out to dinner, but that night when I went to pick her up, she said she wanted to make dinner for us.

"OK," I said, hoping the smile on my face didn't look as fake as it felt. My previous girlfriends had attempted this, but it never worked. I'd choke down dinner as fast as possible and lie about how much I enjoyed it.

Shelley brought out fried chicken, mashed potatoes, and green beans. I took one bite and said, "Will you marry me?" We had a good laugh and were both relieved that I loved her cooking so much. When it was time for dessert, she brought out homemade chocolate cake. I said, "I'm not kidding anymore, goddamn it. Marry me."

Having someone cook for you *and* sleep with you, willingly—without the use of blackmail or chloroform—it's like winning the lottery. But lottery winners can lose all sense of proportion, which is what happened to me.

Food makes us happy. We're just wired that way. We celebrate over burgers, and we commiserate over deep-fried Twinkies wrapped in bacon and slathered in hot fudge and whipped cream.

What, you don't?

In the formative years of our relationship, we bonded over barbecue, pizza, Spaghetti Warehouse—when we could afford it—and anyplace that served a bitchin' plate of cheese fries.

I ate a lot when we moved to Amarillo. I hated the place, and I was depressed. I didn't know how to control my emotions or desires. I was disappointed with my direction in life, so I took it out on my wife by making her feel guilty, which made me feel bad for being so petty.

I ate my way through my feelings. Can't find a job to work between tours? *How about some Oreo cake balls?* Can't find any decent guys to jam with? *Mexican casserole, here I come.* Can't have a conversation unless it involves God, guns, and football? *Screw it. I'm going to Dyer's for the Cowboy Special.*

Then throw in armadillo eggs—jalapeños stuffed with cheese and rolled in a batter of sausage, Bisquick, and more cheese—and you can see that I was headed for trouble.

One day a friend and I made a bet over a hockey game. He likes the Colorado Avalanche; I like the Dallas Stars. If Dallas won, he'd have to wear my Stars jersey. If Colorado won, I'd have to wear his Avs jersey.

The Stars that night were not big and bright, so I wound up in that stupid Avs jersey. My buddy took a picture and showed me. I couldn't believe what I saw. Forget the jersey. I was fat. When did this happen? Why didn't anyone tell me?

We all have moments like this. One day you're running a 5K. The next thing you know, you're a fat guy in an Avs jersey. What now? Shit, at that point I was still in my thirties.

It hit me hard. I kept thinking of my dad. His poor health hurt my mom and cost him his life way too soon. He did finally lose weight. He used the method called colon cancer. So . . . fuck that. I was in a bad place, and I knew I couldn't keep doing that to myself—or to my wife. If I had kept going, where would I be now? It's not like your metabolism gets any faster when you hit forty.

Of course, the other factor here is that I play in a rock band. I'm not totally vain, but I do feel a responsibility to look somewhat respectable onstage.

If you're around my age and you care about music, you've probably noticed a lot of our old heroes aren't looking too good these days. I'm not talking about getting older. Everybody gets older. So your hair is thinner. So you have some lines on your face. Can you still play? Can you still write a good song? Then hit it.

But when you hit three hundred pounds . . . shit, that's a different kind of rock and roll altogether.

As it turned out, the very week I saw that photo of fat Doni, I met Barry, the first martial arts instructor and training partner of my adult life. You know the old line that begins "When the student is ready"? We started working out together, and, as I said, in two months, I lost thirty pounds. I don't want to say it was easy, but it was fast.

There you go. It's Donivan's Miracle Martial Arts Diet, and it might just work for you.

I do still love to eat. I'm not going to preach and pretend I'm a health freak 100 percent of the time. I went vegetarian for five years but decided to put meat back in my diet for protein. Now I just try to eat with a conscience about what I'm putting in my body. I can still go to Dyer's from time to time. I can still indulge in the occasional Oreo cake ball. It's all about maintaining balance.

That is the Dao of armadillo eggs.

GARAGE DAYS REVISITED

MUSICIANS HAVE a special appreciation for garages. They're our first practice spaces and rehearsal halls. Most moms will not tolerate all that racket in the house, so you have your dad pull the cars out, and you shove the lawnmower aside to make room for the band. Later, the garage becomes your first recording studio. My brother and I were actually allowed to practice in the house, but we did our time in garage bands. We know a little about garages.

When I returned to martial arts, I knew I needed a place to work out at home. If you train only when class is in session, you'll be limiting yourself to a few hours a week, and you won't get very far like that, even if your teacher is Lei Kung the Thunderer. I cleared a space in the garage, and I've been training there ever since. It's my dojang away from the grandmaster's.

A dojang doesn't need to be a shrine. No marble, glass, or flute music required. It should be austere and quiet so you can focus. The garage fits the bill. It probably already smells funky too, so you

In the garage with my first band, Rattlehead. It was 1988, a good year for metal. That's Rob Tate to my left and Michael Richardson to my right.

can sweat everywhere, and it's not going to matter. As you read this, an army of martial artists is training in garages around the world.

The one I'm working out in now was built in 1928. That's pretty awesome if you stop to think about it—a garage that's approaching a hundred years old. It survived the Dust Bowl. It was here when Woody Guthrie passed through Amarillo, John Steinbeck too. Its freshest coat of paint came when Truman was president. Now that paint is chipped and cracking, and pieces of it have blown away.

The garage-door opener doesn't always work, so sometimes I have to get in through the dilapidated side door, which I hold closed with a bungee cord. I force my way in. The place smells of old wood, and the attic is falling in from decades of Panhandle winters.

When we moved into the house, the garage was still piled with crap. The shelves along the back wall were filled with old paint, boards, and tile. In one of the squares I found a briefcase that was at least fifty years old. It contained yellowed survey plans. The property used to have a bigger lot with a chicken coop out back. A previous owner had glued the Jesus fish emblem inside one of the cabinet doors. In the next one over, he glued a *Playboy* pinup. We give you thanks and praise.

The grease-stained concrete floor is cold even in the summer. I work out in bare feet, and my soles are black by the end. The hard floor is not the best for my knees. I should get a mat. I've also been battling an awful case of fungus on my left foot. The nails are thick and look like soap, but the fragrance is not like soap.

Sorry. I know it's disgusting. It's a sacrifice I've made for taekwondo.

I'm sure my fellow classmates have noticed my frankenfoot. If I graze someone in class, he'll have to get treated for syphilis.

I'll leave it at that. For further research, check out the Zappa song "Stink-Foot."

I work out in the garage morning and night, and, inch by labored inch, I advance on this martial path. I have a long way to go, but I can say I've progressed, turning into something more than a forty-one-year-old barista. I like that the old garage is the site of that transformation.

In 2008, when I was preparing for my audition with the Toadies, I went to the same garage to prepare.

I found out their bass spot was open, and I decided to go for it. It seemed like a long shot, but then much of what you really want in life is a long shot. I sent an e-mail through the band's website, and they wrote back to set up a meeting.

"I already got an audition?" I thought. "Shit, that was easy. I'm going to nail this." As I read on, my confidence withered. They said it is a "pick gig," "downstrokes only."

My reply: "No problem. Got it." I was lying my ass off. It *was* a problem.

Fingers or a pick? This is the great dividing line among bassists. There are plenty of awesome pick players—Chris Squire, Inge

Johansson, and Matt Freeman to name a few—but a lot of old-school bassists think the pick is beneath them. They'd never consider using a lowly plectrum. Before the Toadies gig, I'd always felt that way myself.

What's the difference? Pretty much everything. The attack, sustain, tone, muting, phrasing, and technique. Pick playing is brighter, which is good if you're in AC/DC, and you need to cut through two guitars. Fingerstyle tends to be darker and offer greater subtlety.

One advantage of using a pick is that you won't develop blistered carnage where your fingertips used to be. When you're a kid, before you've earned your calluses, your hands get shredded. In those days, having a gig means playing a party at a friend's house. You take the stage—which is probably also a garage—and you're ready to rock the place. Then your blisters break during the first song.

I finally made friends with the pick.

Blisters mad. Arrrrgh. Blisters burst.

You spend the next couple of hours grinding raw fingers into heavy-gauge bass strings. It's fun.

For the Toadies I had to learn a different approach to the instrument. Every day after work I spent an hour or two practicing to the Ramones, AC/DC, and Yes—all pick, all the time. I did that woodshedding in the garage. I keep my basses and amps in the house, but the garage is where you work. I wanted that focus.

I don't get stage fright when I'm playing with the band, but I still get "class fright." Classes make me nervous. Belt tests really freak me out. I practice forms, kicks, and techniques for weeks beforehand, and I practice my breathing to correspond with every move. I go to the dojang ready to nail it. Then the grandmaster walks in, and I forget everything.

"Begin," he says.

Begin what?

My heart pounds. I sweat. I can play music on a big stage in front of thousands, but in my taekwondo class of fifteen or so, my mind goes blank. That's class fright. I'm still new around here. But I draw on my experience as a musician. I know with time, study, and repetition, you can internalize the material. Even complicated patterns become fluent. You can mute the voice of doubt, be present in the moment, and lose yourself in the performance.

There's no holding back onstage. But as a martial artist, when people are around, I'm still a bit of an introvert. I figure no one wants to see some clown in pajamas fighting off invisible attackers and making sounds you only hear when your dad is on the can. I spare my neighbors the horror show and work out in seclusion.

No one can see me in the garage. In the garage I go all out.

SPARRING WITH OWEN

WELL, I knew this would happen. It's why I worried about sparring with these goddamn kids. I was pretty sure Owen broke my leg.

It was sparring night, so we put on the pads. We wear arm guards and shin guards made of molded foam, headgear, and a chest pad that reminds me of a bulletproof vest, only this one has a big red circle that screams HIT ME HERE.

Owen was my first opponent. He's a special kid. Ask him how he's doing, and he'll reply, "I've been working on my kicks." Not "I'm doing well." Not "Fine. How are you?" It's just, "I've been working on my kicks."

Right.

Kicking is pretty much the only thing he works on, but, as I've said, holy shit can he kick. Before class he was kicking a hanging bag that weighs 150 pounds. One shot and he makes it swing with ease. When I saw that, I thought, "Man, I wouldn't want to face those mutant kicks. I'm glad I'm not sparring with Owen."

Then the grandmaster yelled, "Donivan, spar with Owen!" Except the words came out of his mouth in slow motion. I watched them ooze forth and heard them, but I tried not to think of the hanging bag or what this kid would do to me. Or the mess I'd just made in my underwear.

On to our bout:

In this corner, wearing the white dobok with the red belt, official weight 170 pounds, kicking ass and forgetting to take names, the Kool-Aid Kid, Owen Smith.

And in this corner, wearing the white dobok with the orange belt; official weight 165 pounds; the purveyor of low-end frequencies; the Bengay Kid; the fighting pride of Sherman, Texas; Donivan Blair.

We faced each other, bowed, and Owen came gunning for me. Sparring is not supposed to be combat—you mainly try to tap the opponent—but this kid can't seem to grasp that. He chopped away at my thigh, and it was all I could do to stay upright. My bones and musculature cried out. I took five minutes of that.

Then I went up against two more opponents, both black belts. After the third I could no longer stand on my left leg. My entire thigh was numb and getting worse by the second. I could actually feel the swelling grow.

In an act of mercy, the grandmaster allowed me to sit out the next round. My vision began to swim, my heart raced, and I was sweating like mad. "Here it comes," I thought, "the heart attack that finally does me in."

I just wanted to leave the school and drop dead in my car, but I'm guilty of being a macho asshole from time to time, so I hung around and acted like it didn't hurt me that bad.

Once I got home I hobbled into the house, took a bath, and waited for the hurt to go down. And I kept waiting. And waiting.

I took Shelley's advice and went to an emergency care center for an X-ray. The doctor told me it was just a bad bruise. The good news was that Owen didn't break it. The bad news was that the kick went through my quad and struck bone. Shelley had to tell me the rest because I fainted when he said "struck bone." My kryptonite is broken bones—and apparently even bruised ones. Want to take me out? Tell me about that time you blew your kneecap skating, and I'm De Niro in *Raging Bull*.

The doctor said to stay off it and rest for two to three weeks. I can be a stubborn, impatient OCD dick, so I was thinking of ways to continue my training during those two to three weeks.

Well, he didn't say I couldn't work out with my right leg.

Important lessons here:

1. Get out of the way.
2. Learn to block better.
3. Sparring with kids still sucks. I wouldn't try to hurt a teenager, but to a teenager an adult looks like a trophy.
4. Taekwondo is vital to me. Reaching black belt would be one of the major accomplishments of my life, but I don't want it to take my whole life. I can't make much progress when I'm injured.
5. Downtime sucks. I have to stay healthy because being on injured reserve is un-fucking-bearable.

After two weeks away, I felt better and returned to the dojang. Of course, the first person I ran into was Owen.

"Have you been training?" he said.

"No."

"Why haven't you been training?" he said.

"I injured my leg two weeks ago in sparring."

"You did?"

"Yeah. You were the one who injured me."

"Oh," he said. "I've been working on my kicks."

Yeah, no shit.

WWCND?

To BE, or not to be: that is *not* the question. The real question here is what would Chuck Norris do?

I know our heroes get hurt. Sometimes they need surgery and months of physical therapy. But no one ever shows us that story. We only see the best at their best. That's the magic of Hollywood. In Amarillo we have no magic. In Amarillo it's just brutal realism.

My left leg is still killing me. I'm still limping. I move like a fat old man, waddling from side to side instead of actually moving forward. On Monday I visited the grandmaster and told him I'd be back in a week. I did the same thing last week, but my leg is still not ready. In the meantime, I'm trying to keep up my training at home. I'm on a strict regimen of self-doubt, whimpering, and ibuprofen.

I've retreated to the garage to be alone. This is my usual training spot, but this is not my usual training. I'm focusing on techniques that don't require much from the left leg, and that eliminates a lot of my workout. It isn't satisfying, but I'm doing what I can.

What would Chuck Norris do? Would he fight through this? Would he take time off to rest and heal? It's so damn difficult to take time off. Holding still gives me fits of anxiety and feelings of worthlessness. I haven't been at taekwondo that long. If I stop training for two or three weeks, I may never return. At least that's my fear. I wish I could give Chuck a call for some advice.

People goof on Chuck, and the internet is full of jokes about him. You know the kind:

When Chuck Norris was born, he drove his mom home from the hospital.

Chuck Norris is the reason Waldo is hiding.

Chuck Norris counted to infinity. Twice.

It's funny stuff, but the guy is still a barometer in my martial arts life. I look up to him. I'm not big on super-conservative Chuck; I prefer the Chuck Norris of the seventies and early eighties. Hell, even *Walker, Texas Ranger* is a favorite. He carries a gun, but he doesn't need it when he can just kick bad guys in the face.

I relate to Chuck because he seems like a real guy. Bruce Lee was otherworldly, with superpowers unknown to mere mortals. Would you like to be that good? Forget it. Chuck, on the other hand, just worked hard. He showed that you can get somewhere even if you are a kid from nowhere. He didn't need a stunt double, but an acting double might have helped. I couldn't see that when I was ten. Now I see it, but I don't care.

I think Chuck would tell me to push ahead. I can't hold back. I'm supposed to test for yellow belt soon.

If I put together a training montage of the last week or so, it would look like this:

In one clip after another I am training hard in a dusky gym. I'm sweating, using one leg to kick the heavy bag. I'm surrounded by exercise equipment and grime. I'm injured and getting nowhere. See that look of frustration?

I'm wearing a headband. I never wear headbands, but we'll just go with it. You become aware that time is passing in the montage because my clothes change—except for the headband, of course. Always with the headband.

Enjoy the bad eighties rock music. It features plenty of synth, a Gibson Flying V, a LynnDrum, and a Steinberger L-series bass. The lyrics go like this: "Just because Owen nearly broke your leg / You don't need to be a pirate with a wooden peg / Ooooh, go for it / Never give up / You gotta go for it."

Now I'm in a sparring session with my training partner. I glance to the corner and see the grandmaster. He mouths, "You can do it." I shake my head. No, I can't. My partner pounds me. The grandmaster says, "Come on, Donivan. You just have to believe."

Those are the magic words. The look in my eye tells you that yes, yes, I do believe. I break through the pain and uncertainty and kick with my left leg. I blast my training partner across the ring.

I can do it. I raise my fist in triumph.

I'm back, bitches. Let me at those Commies.

That's what Chuck Norris would do.

AMARILLO BELT

MY YELLOW-BELT test is tomorrow. I *believe* I'm prepared, but then again, some people believe the Earth is six thousand years old, so watch out for belief.

I know all the material for my test. I could go in there and nail it, or I could totally blow it. A lifetime of performing has taught me that I will be somewhere between those two extremes. You always fall short of perfection, but, with the right preparation, you still land somewhere pretty good. And anyway, if I do blow it, I'll just learn and adjust. Pretty simple, right?

It wasn't always that simple. I have a history of making everything so damn complicated. I'll blame the OCD. I get stuck on something, and it becomes a scab I just can't stop picking.

That's always been my way, but I feel like I've adopted a new mindset since I started training with the grandmaster. How do I describe it? I am as obsessed as ever, but I just might have found a tad more patience. I think I'm getting better at considering the long view.

Training is awesome for all the reasons I expected, but lately I've become aware of a few I didn't expect. One has to do with music. It's been my focus since I was a kid. Who am I playing with? What are we writing? When are we recording? How long is the tour? For the past few months, my life has been all taekwondo all the time. Working on strikes and forms has taken the place of learning Rush songs, and you know what? For the first time in a long time, I am content.

I'm not complacent about music, and I'm sure not giving up. I just don't feel that obsession to prove myself. I can play my instrument and enjoy it, and that's enough. It's a breakthrough.

When I started at the local WTF affiliate, I worried that I'd fall down and look like an idiot. Now when I fall down and look like an idiot, I just get up. Big damn deal. I don't mean to make it as simple as "try, try again," but it's just about perseverance. There's no magic to it.

Here's another unexpected benefit of my training. It's allowed me to accept Amarillo, at least a little more. Don't get me wrong: I'd still change a lot about this place if I could, but I am no longer consumed with hatred for it. When we arrived here in 2000, I felt I had failed. I've talked about this, and I won't belabor the point. I had devoted my entire life to music, and then I turned up in a town that doesn't give a good cow shit about it.

But all these years later, I am still here. I have the gig with the Toadies, Shelley and I have a house we love, and now I belong to a taekwondo school. I like that place and the characters I train with there.

So fuck it. I am an Amarilloan, goddamn it.

*　　*　　*

Yellow belt acquired. Test nights can be pretty involved, but tonight there were just three of us, and it went fast.

You have to pay extra for a belt test. Schools everywhere do this. Shelley asked, "What happens if you pay and don't pass?" I said you don't get the rank, and you're out the money. I think that's fair. You should have a little something on the line, something more than just pride. I don't want to buy my way to black. I'd think no one would, but there are mail-order programs that work that way. Send money, go at your own pace, send more money, and they send you a black belt. Then you can wipe your ass with it.

Running a martial arts studio is a business. I get it. It takes money to keep the lights on, and if an instructor is an expert, he deserves to make a living teaching the art he's spent his life working on. But just once I would like to see someone pay up front and fail a belt test. Especially if I am that person. I would sacrifice that money just to know the system is legit.

Is the grandmaster all about the money? No. Not for a minute do I think that. He's an incredible martial artist, a great teacher, and a very hard man to please. But he does have a business to run. If you fail students when they don't deliver on their tests, fewer of them will advance in rank. They will leave and take their money with them.

Why the cynicism? I've reached another checkpoint on a long road, and I should be happy, but I can't get over this tendency to doubt myself. Some voice in my head says, "What if you really do suck? What if this school is a sham?" I wonder about that even though I've seen no evidence of it.

I know I just wrote about feeling content with my training, but I'm not feeling it tonight. I misunderstood the grandmaster during the test and performed the wrong kick. I also needed two tries to break a board with a side kick. Should I have failed? I don't know if I would have allowed me to advance, but then again I'm not the teacher. I'm just some forty-one-year-old asshole.

The real training is about to begin. My leg is finally back to normal, and as long as I don't have to spar with the Tasmanian Owen again, it should stay that way. My cardio is in dire need of improvement, and my legs need to get stronger. I couldn't really kick when I was injured, and my calves and thighs feel weak for it.

At the end of the night, once we had passed our tests, the grand-master asked the three of us what we've learned from taekwondo. When my turn came, I said, "Perseverance and determination." If I learn only those two things, then my time with him will be a success. But another long-term goal is to kill this self-doubt.

UNITY OR SOMETHING LIKE IT

S TOP ME if you've heard this one.

Two bulls, father and son, are at the top of a hill, looking down on a herd of cows grazing in a pasture. The son looks at his dad and says, "I got an idea. Let's run down there and fuck us one of them cows."

The dad turns to him and says, "How 'bout we *walk* down and fuck *all* of them?"

That's a little Texas humor for you. It's all about the difference age and experience make, and I think of it every night when we run in class. As I've said, before instruction begins, we have to complete twenty laps around the main mat, ten one way, ten the other. Let this be known: I cannot stand running. I ran a lot when I was younger, mainly because somebody was always trying to beat the shit out of me. Why? I was a sarcastic little asshole. Acerbic wit was my weapon of choice.

Remember the days of awkward boners? I do. Somebody in my

class would point out the tent in my pants, and I'd say, "That's OK. Your mom doesn't mind."

Out came the fists.

I tell ya, life ain't easy for a boy named Doni.

About the time I hit twelve years old, I stopped running and stayed to fight. I got pounded, but at least I didn't have to freaking run.

As much as I do hate running, it's great for cardio, especially for taekwondo, so I run like an idiot every class. But unlike my fellow classmates, I'm an idiot with a plan: I pace myself. They sprint on by. I keep jogging, slow and steady, like the old guy I am. You can probably guess how this is going to turn out.

At the end of the night, when it's time for conditioning, the kids are gassed, but I still have a little in the tank. This happens every single class. These kids are incapable of learning. I don't know much about history, don't know much biology, but what I do know is teenage boys are dumbasses. They get in a pack, start competing with one another, and lose all sense of foresight and restraint.

When it comes to sparring, they are no less enthusiastic. I'm pretty sure sparring is for instruction, not destruction, but there's no telling them that. Even if they have their school pictures the next day.

I do see advantages to working out with them though. Train with students who are younger and in better shape, and you'll be a killer if you have to fight someone your own age. That round-house might not impress an eighteen-year-old, but it will sure as hell knock the crap out of a forty-year-old.

At the other extreme—the Centrum end of the spectrum—we have Dawn and Ray. At least we used to have them. I haven't seen much of those two lately. They are husband and wife, both black belts in their fifties, and both way past their due date. They are the taekwondo version of Laurel and Hardy. If they could ever kick high—or low for that matter—you wouldn't know it now. They have the bearing of haughty old teachers. They're above everything we do, but they'll deign to take part nonetheless, perhaps for our edification. Put all this together, and you have the perfect mix for physical comedy. That's just what their workouts are.

Their main motivation for attending class is to yell at the rest of us. Their bodies have failed them, but their mouths still work at the black-belt level, so they have to get in there and kick ass.

Taekwondo seems to be an activity they do together for fun. I have a problem with this. Taekwondo is not an activity. Taekwondo is not fun. Taekwondo has a purpose. What is that purpose? Right now I cannot say. In the words of the Magic 8 Ball, "Ask again later."

The good part of having Dawn and Ray around is that they make me look like an actual runner. They just putter along at a brisk pace. They're like mall walkers but adorned in pajamas with a garish belt. Well, mall walkers.

I have to yuck it up now. I'm about ten years from joining them in front of Auntie Anne's.

I'm already on my way down that path. The young 'uns grab their uniforms and run off to class, but I can't take part without a compression brace for my right knee and shitloads of Doan's back pills. Every morning after class night I limp for an hour because my left heel is ablaze. I should probably get that looked at.

Maybe I should get my head checked too. I'm destroying my body, and it doesn't appear to concern me—and that is what concerns me. Explode now and worry about later . . . later. Look at it this way, and I'm not so different from the teenagers in my class. That's a depressing thought.

All these ailments should make a sane person take up something more appropriate for his age. Stamp collecting, for example. Or model trains. They're cool.

I am giving this my all and logging a lot of hours, and I'd like to think I'm more committed than your average weekend warrior, but sometimes I see through that illusion. I tell the grandmaster about my rigorous solo workouts, and I can almost hear what he's thinking: "Great, Doni. The Kukkiwon will be calling you soon for pointers."

The Kukkiwon in Seoul is the world headquarters of taekwondo. If you knew that, my joke probably packed more punch.

The grandmaster has told stories about his first taekwondo lessons as a kid in Korea. He was five years old. His master had the children place their heads on the ground and walk in circles. He wanted to make them as dizzy as possible. It was the first step toward improving their equilibrium.

The grandmaster said around that age, students lie on the floor with an adult standing on either side. Each takes a leg and pulls. Imagine putting the kid in a split, but then going way farther. They keep going until they break the musculature and tendons. A bit uncomfortable perhaps, but when the kid heals, he's able to kick higher than any human being should.

Don't try that one at your American school.

When you go through that kind of shit—at five years old no less—and then some dumb rocker dude tells you he had a good training day doing fifty kicks in his garage you have every right to roll your eyes.

Despite all the taekwondo schools in the world, despite all the organizations and governing bodies, not one person owns this art. It's everyone's, and in that way, it is no one's.

You can say the same for music. We all love it. Many of us create it. We listen together, and we listen alone. We can say what music seems to be, but no single person holds the definition of what it is. There's something magical about that.

You can divide my taekwondo class by age, ability, and culture. We come from different times and places. We're at different stages of life, we have different methods, and we have different goals. We don't enjoy the same food or films or books, and we sure don't like the same music. And yet taekwondo unites us.

Maybe *unites* is too strong a word.

And yet taekwondo makes us associates.

There. That's better.

VASECTOMY: THE BEST DECISION I EVER MADE

I DON'T HAVE what you call parental instincts. Never have, never will. Changing dirty diapers and being thrown up on are activities for far stronger men. When Shelley and I first got married, we decided to give our fledgling union at least five years before we even thought about children. It was fun going through the motions, but thankfully nothing ever came of our endeavors.

We did have our scares. I remember more than once being on the phone with her and feeling chills when hearing the news that she had missed her period.

"Well, we're going to be parents, grown-ups now."

"Yeah. Have to get a crib."

"Paint the kid's room."

"Time to buck up and be a man," I'd tell myself. "I'm going to be a father. Oh God, I feel sorry for this kid."

In a week or so she'd find out she actually wasn't pregnant. She'd tell me the great news, and we'd celebrate with more sex. It was a vicious cycle.

After thirteen years of marriage we decided we were still not ready to be parents. We tended to spend our money on travel, tattoos, bass guitars, and Legos, and we liked it that way. What would we do with a kid? Everyone knows kids hate Legos.

Toward the end of that year, Shelley was looking at our health-insurance statement. We'd made a few visits to the doctor, and she noticed that we'd met our deductible.

"Hey," she said, "want to get a vasectomy?" This sweet, gorgeous farm girl with no evil in her wanted me to get my nuts cut. "It's free," she added.

She pointed out that a vasectomy is less invasive than a tubal ligation. If I went through with it, we'd never have another scare again. What did I think?

I thought, "Holy shit. I'm going to be a hero. Think of all the hero sex I'll get."

I was thirty-eight at the time, but I was pretty much thirteen at heart. I still am. I can't get past the fact that I have twenty-four-hour access to boobs, for life. A quick snip would ensure that no screaming interloper would ever get in the way. When you think of it like that, who can resist?

It was already November, and if we were going to get this done gratis, I had to get in before the end of the year. We made the call, and I spoke to a nurse.

"How many children do you have?" she asked.

"None, and we want to keep it that way."

"Well, we're not going to do it."

Not going to do it? Did I hear that right? She repeated her answer. What the ever-loving fuck?

They wouldn't perform a vasectomy on a guy who had no kids. They figured most marriages would fail anyway, so after our inevitable divorce, I would remarry—more boobs—and, this is a whole lot of supposition, but at that point I'd want to have kids. Because everyone wants children, and if you don't procreate, there's something wrong with you.

They assumed my wife was the one keeping us from sprinkling the kids everywhere.

Shelley grabbed the phone and handled it with a few terse words. Then Nurse Ratched got us an appointment with a different doctor, one who didn't mind keeping Blair progeny from ever walking the face of the Earth.

Humanity, you're welcome.

I make light of this, but it is a big decision, not bringing life into the world. We were bucking a convention of marriage— arguably *the* convention of marriage. I have some idea of what it takes to be a good father, and I also know I don't have that in me.

When we told our families, I expected a bigger fight, but they pretty much said, "Yeah. We figured." I was thankful they understood. Then some part of me was offended.

"Wait," I thought. "You think we can't do it? You think we wouldn't make good parents?"

Snipping day arrived. The nurse led me to the procedure room, and I met my doctor, a dead ringer for the comic Kevin Nealon. I asked how long it would take.

"Not more than an hour," he said. "Gotta keep it quick. I'm grabbing a flight to Vegas to see the Black Crowes this weekend." The man had his priorities. My balls were in his hands.

His assistant was shaving me—not my face—and we were talking about rock and roll. Because that's what you do. I mentioned that I'm in the Toadies, and he stopped cold with the razor, looked me in the eye, and said, "Man, that's badass."

Twenty minutes later I was on my way home. I was a hero, albeit a hero who would spend the weekend with a bag of frozen peas on his testicles. I'd sink into the comforts of home: comics, video games, and a Blue Sky cheeseburger, an Amarillo favorite.

We made it. We never had kids, and now we never would. I declared that the best day of my life.

"Really?" Shelley said. "How about the day we got married?"

"Yeah. That was pretty good too."

Why am I sharing all of this? Well, I do like talking about my balls, but it really does relate to the martial arts.

The grandmaster requires students on the path to black belt to take on additional responsibilities at the dojang, and one of those includes teaching new students. We will be the ones instructing the future of taekwondo, and we need to prepare for that. I thought he might ask me to work with some of the teenagers who needed help with the basics. I figured I might even enjoy it.

One day he called me into his office. He did have an assignment for me, but it wasn't quite what I had in mind. He told me I'd be responsible for the after-school kids, ages five through twelve. I'd take the van, pick them up, and drive them to the dojang. Then I'd lead their workout.

Please kill me.

Like many dojangs in America, ours has an after-school program. It's part day care, part gym. The van makes a lot of stops because we have kids from several elementary and junior high schools.

Every one of these kids is crazy. From the minute they get in the van until I deposit them at the school, they scream like little girls. No amount of chiding will deter them. They flail around, hit one another, and make me want to drive into oncoming traffic just for some peace and quiet.

No, I'm kidding. That would be wrong.

Mostly.

Boys at this age have limitless energy, especially when they are doing something annoying. My brother and I were a pair of Tasmanian devils, so I get it. School finally gets out for the day. You've been cramped up, and now you're free. You and your buddies are on your way to the taekwondo school. Time to go crazy.

Lois, the senior student who runs the school for the grandmaster, offered a little advice on dealing with the kids. She told me I could never let them see me sweat.

"You have to be firm from the get-go," she said. "If they think they can get one by you, you're toast."

I've heard similar instructions on handling wild animals at the zoo—or dealing with inmates in prison. Just drop the biggest guy in the yard. That's the only way you get respect.

I scoffed, thinking, "That's nuts. They're just kids." No, she was right. By the end of the first day I had to bounce a third grader with a big mouth. She shouldn't have called me Yellow Teeth.

The grandmaster drove on that first outing. He is a man of tremendous discipline, but even men of tremendous discipline mumble under their breath. It was all in Korean, so I have no idea what he said, but it didn't sound good, I'll tell you that.

He showed me the route to take and which children to pick up. I tried to remember them by location because they all looked alike to me. With my luck I would end up kidnapping some strange kid and spending the rest of my days in the joint, where I would, of course, have to drop the biggest guy in the yard. Talk about full circle.

After a few days the grandmaster was away, and I was on my own with the after-school program. By the way, kids can smell fear.

I felt like I'd been dropped into *Planet of the Apes*, where the monkeys have taken over, destroyed cars, thrown feces everywhere, and started their own government. They were running amok. I tried to call the group to order.

"Hey, guys," I said. No reply.

"All right, listen up, everyone." Nothing.

So I yelled in my loudest voice: "*Charyhut!*" That's the Korean command to stand at attention with your hands at your sides— exactly what they did. Amazing. The power I had. I felt like Dr. Doom.

That lasted for about a second. Soon they were at one another's throats again, running around like ants in a bag of Pixy Stix. Several times the kids asked if they could play dodgeball, as if this were recess. I'm not a phys. ed. teacher, and I hate dodgeball. These kids' parents were paying for taekwondo, and by God taekwondo they would get.

I ran them. Hard. It was awesome. Punch. Kick. Block. Repeat. I had them sweating, panting, almost throwing up—but more on that part later. If exhausting children through physical activity is cool, then I'm Miles Davis.

After a week of that, things were going well. The kids were responding to me, and we were getting along. Sometimes I would think, "I'm getting the hang of this."

One day when I was out with the van, I picked up a kid we'll call Quinn. He said, "I don't feel so good." I pretty much ignored him. There's a lesson here.

After a few more stops I heard a collective "Yew" from the backseat. Quinn had puked on himself, on the seat, on his book bag, and on the other kids. Everybody knows puking is contagious. The chain reaction began, and the rest of the ride was a taekwondo pukefest.

When we got to the dojang, all the kids were biohazards and the van was ready for quarantine. Quinn was crying, covered in snot and puke, and holding a little bear he had brought from home. He'd puked on the bear too.

I said I don't have parental instincts. At that moment, I must confess, something stirred deep within me. I looked at that poor kid and his sad little stuffed animal, and I thought, "Well, there you have it: the reason I got a vasectomy."

Then I cleaned up the puke. Perseverance is one of the main qualities of taekwondo. It might sound kind of silly, but I drew from that the whole time.

When I set out on this martial adventure, I would have never imagined myself in that situation, but there was no point in fighting it. Sweeping the dojang or cleaning up pukey kids is part of the path. You have to take ownership of the school and look out for those who train there with you.

And anyway, the kids weren't bad, even when they were freaking out and begging to play dodgeball. They were just kids.

A seven-year-old doesn't know any better. He's just a lump of crazy in the shape of a kid.

When the kids did pay attention and I was actually able to teach them something, it was an amazing feeling. All these bruises and broken bones were worth it if I could show just one kid how to do a decent roundhouse kick.

I went home that night feeling pretty good about the day, despite all the grossness. Then Shelley told me we were having goulash for dinner. I threw up.

MIDLIFE CRISIS

H ERE'S A novel idea for you: this whole martial arts endeavor is
just proof of my midlife crisis. I could shut up and endure it,
but instead I'm documenting it with X-rays and medical bills—not
to mention a book. I'm past my prime, and my life's in a tailspin,
so I'm paying to have sixteen-year-olds kick me in the face. It's a
pathetic attempt to recapture my lost youth.

Well, isn't that just the elephant in the fucking dojang?

I will say this: something happens when you hit forty. You realize
half your life is behind you and begin to wonder if you've spent it
right. Thoughts of failures and missed opportunities float in on
clouds of doubt. You make changes inside and out.

My wife is a good Christian farm girl. I'm sure some people
wonder what she's doing with taekwonDoni and his potty mouth.
She got her first tattoo at forty-one, and now she has both arms
sleeved out. Crisis? Nah, it's just about reaching an age where
you say, "Fuck it. I'm going to do whatever I want with my life."

That's where I am now. Call it a crisis if you want. I don't care. I'm busy getting kicked in the face.

I thought of a way to make the abuse even worse. I want to fight in a tournament. Am I a natural pugilist? No. Are my friends noticing my quick reflexes? Not exactly. No one thinks I will do well in a tournament. Even I don't think I'll do very well, but that's exactly why I want to try. I don't need a trophy; I just want the experience.

As I've gotten interested in martial arts and combat sports, I've gravitated toward films and documentaries about fighters. I'm thinking of *Southpaw* with Jake Gyllenhaal; *Warrior* with Tom Hardy and Joel Edgerton; and a great doc called *Mexican Fighter*, about Cain Velasquez.

As a rule these stories depict hardcore badasses who have an innate drive to fight. They push themselves, get faster, grow stronger, and go further. I identify with that drive, but it seems for all the fighters, those are just the means to their ultimate goal: to destroy the other guy. I don't identify with that. You need killer instinct to fight, and as I've gotten older, I've realized I just don't have it. I wish I did.

At least I think I wish that. But if you're that kind of person, you're probably that kind of person all the time, and it must influence where you go, what you do, and who you interact with. It definitely influences who will put up with you.

So now I don't know: do I want killer instinct? This is getting complicated.

Let me start again. I like films about fighters, but I can't really identify with the combatants. What does inspire me is the training. I love the idea of doing that much work to prepare for a critical moment. You have a major test ahead, and you know that, win or lose, you will have made an incredible journey and stretched your limits. You'll never be the same.

I don't have a camera guy and a boom op following me around, but I want a little taste of this. Competing in a tournament will push me out of my routines, and I need that. If I'm not working toward some major goal, I'm afraid I'll end up sitting on my ass all day, playing video games, and getting fat. You know the old saying: "If you don't work hard, the devil will creep in through your vestibulocochlear nerve and make you a fucking loser."

Or something like that. I may have paraphrased.

Some of the grandmaster's students compete in tournaments, and I think it would be cool to join them. I like the idea of loading up, hitting the road, and representing the school. Last year I asked the grandmaster if I could go and compete. I got his usual ten-second pause. Ten uncomfortable seconds. Then he said no.

It's never good to question your master, but what's the deal? I am a big boy. I can even stay out past nine o'clock.

"You make your living with your hands," he said. "I don't want you to injure them."

I wanted to argue, but I couldn't. He was right. Then again, they are *my* hands. I should be able to do what I want with them.

"I'm your master," he added. "I know what's good for you."

That settled it. Maybe he was worried about my hands, or maybe he just didn't think I was ready. Of course I wasn't ready. That's exactly why I wanted to do it. If someone redecorated my face, I'd be richer for the experience. Good enough for me.

Well, a year has passed, and I still want to go to the tournament.

The other night was sparring night, so we put on our assortment of pads, braces, and helmets. The grandmaster ordered me to spar with two opponents. First was the new guy. He has a black belt in kenpo, and he can take care of himself. My next opponent? A ten-year-old kid. What the hell?

That stings. Maybe he just wanted the kid to have the experience, but I couldn't shake the feeling that the grandmaster has little faith in me and what I've learned so far. This hunch only got stronger when I asked him about the upcoming tournament.

"Grandmaster," I said, "may I compete in the tournament next month?"

"Yes," he said.

"In which categories, sir?"

"You may compete in forms and breaking."

"Can I compete in sparring?"

"No."

I assume he meant breaking with kicks. If not, he forgot that business about protecting my hands.

The grandmaster is of the position that men our age are not supposed to spar in tournaments. It's kids' stuff, unseemly for older guys. Black belts, especially older black belts, should spend their time refining their technique and instructing younger students.

I get it, but deep down I have the sense that I'm not good enough. If I could compete in one tournament, I might walk away saying, "He was right. That was a waste of time." But since it's off limits, it just looks all the more interesting.

Some part of me wants to go anyway. I would just enter the tournament as a *ronin*, a samurai with no master. Obviously, I can't do that. I'd never be allowed at the local WTF affiliate again.

I started this chapter with big hope for a tournament story. I thought it would be a freaking riot. But no, this one feels like a loss. I can talk about failures and missed opportunities, about saying, "Fuck it. I'm going to do whatever I want with my life." That is a big part of this martial adventure—which is in no way a midlife crisis, thank you—but the reality is that freedom has its limitations. Some opportunities remain out of reach.

LOST IN TRANSLATION

WE HAVE three new interns visiting the local WTF affiliate. They are from the grandmaster's alma mater in Korea, and they're here to finish their degrees. You can get a bachelor's in taekwondo in Korea. We are so missing the point here.

These three ladies have just arrived in the States, and God help them, Amarillo is their first taste of the country. I can't pronounce any of their names, and I can't spell them either, which makes me a typical American. Let's just call them 실습생들.

Hey, Google says it's right.

실습생들 are, of course, way better than our troupe of clumsy Americans. In fairness, I should say that most of our black belts are fantastic, and they redeem the class. The grandmaster is their instructor, and he doesn't give anyone a pass. But when you consider what separates 실습생들 from the rest of us, you realize it's a chasm we will never cross.

These girls are faster, more powerful, and way more flexible. They're light on their feet, and their motions are graceful, easy, and fluid. I just hope I can steal a little of their skill because I know I'll never catch them. Taekwondo is in their blood and in the fabric of their culture—and when you think of it that way, we are actually the foreign exchange students.

실습생들 are trained not just in kicking, punching, blocking, and hiyahing; they're also trained to teach. While in Amarillo, they get some authentic Texans to straighten out. It's a comedy in the making.

Tonight 실습생들 led the class. They introduced us to some two-man stretches my body just loved. Take for example the one where you stand and your partner squats. You extend your leg and place it on his shoulder, and, little by little, he goes to a standing position. Your leg goes along for the ride, and you get stretched out whether you like it or not. It's painful, but it sure could make you flexible.

We moved on to cardio. 실습생들 led us in SEAL jacks: instead of raising your arms like normal jumping jacks, you wave them in front of your body like a referee signaling that a field goal is no good. Try it for yourself. It will probably exhaust and deplete you too. It turns out 실습생들 graduate with honors if they kill an American during training. They did not succeed tonight, but there's always next time.

Then they led us through kicks. In one of the drills, we kicked at ankle height and then head height, but we did this at the tempo of oh, say, "Overkill," by Motörhead. We looked like the Taekwondo City Rockettes on speed.

We followed this blitzkrieg with . . . more kicks, of course. We lay on the floor, stretched our legs up, and went through round-house, side, and front kicks, but this time we did them in slow motion—more like the tempo of "Black Sabbath," by Black Sabbath—from the record *Black Sabbath*. (Come on, guys.)

When all of that was over, we were finished with the warm-up. The fucking warm-up.

I couldn't help but wonder what 실습생들 think when watching us lower belts. We just don't have the form or flexibility to execute the strokes and strikes. We are, well, shitty. I think that's the word in your language. The average five-year-old kid back in Korea is already better than I am. Not only do the kids have better technique but they are more dedicated to the art. Most American children cannot be bothered to turn off the video game and practice Taegeuk 1; meanwhile, their Korean counterparts are advancing in Koryo and have already earned their black belts.

I don't think I'm just romanticizing about Korea. Have you seen American kids lately? They're fucking fat.

More cultural generalizations, you say? Don't mind if I do. Koreans put immense value on discipline, training, knowledge, and getting into a university. This is the way to better oneself. Americans put immense value on shortcuts, skimming, appearance, and getting by. This is the way to get a job at daddy's firm.

Korea: You better be the best, in college and in the rest of your life, because you have a million people in line behind you, ready to take your place.

United States: Are Johnny's grades good enough so he can play in Friday's game? What will we do without our starting quarterback?

Korea: Honor your ancestors and your masters.

United States: You're telling me I can't take my Glock into Starbucks? You, sir, will see me on Facebook.

실습생들 will get some taste of this dumb shit on their way to earning their degrees in taekwondo. And I do mean earning.

A degree in taekwondo. I still can't get over it. If I weren't so damn old, I would sell everything, move to Korea, and apply for the taekwondo program. Even if I got fat on Korean barbeque, even if I got out with a C+ and brought great shame to my instructors and classmates, I could still return to the States a badass.

OCD: BETTER THAN COFFEE
ANY DAY

ONE GOOD thing about having obsessive-compulsive disorder: you get shit done. If you have OCD and you feel the need to do something about it, you could take prescription meds or go off for counseling. Or you could study a musical instrument, climb Mt. Kilimanjaro, build a house by hand, take flying lessons, lay a hundred miles of railroad track, earn a PhD, run a marathon, write a book, and become a black belt—all in the same day.

Shit, all in the same sentence.

In the words of my editor Doran, "OCD needs to be reclassified as a superpower."

I'd like to say I am highly motivated and intelligent, but I'm neither. Whatever I accomplish, I do for one simple reason: I can't deal with sitting on my ass. *The voice* will not allow me to rest, at least not until I've met all its demands. If you've heard the voice, you know exactly what I mean. If you haven't, you probably think I am mental.

The voice is a dictator. It commands you to meet all its requirements and complete every task. It might tell you to check the stove over and over, even when deep down you know it's off. It might force you out of bed a dozen times to make sure the door is locked, even though you knew it was all along. The voice might insist that you say a magic word a certain number of times. The voice is counting. The voice always knows.

My voice sounds just like Ethyl Merman. There's no ignoring that.

My mom first observed OCD in me when I was a little kid. I couldn't stop touching the wall, and I had to count how many times I did it. We might have had places to go and important shit to do, but there I was, stuck and unable to walk away: "Nineteen, twenty, twenty-one, twenty-two . . . ."

I had other equally maddening tendencies. My mom called these my "habits," and they made me a target in my own house. My family meant no harm, but sometimes they couldn't stand any more. I get it. What do you do with a kid who has to do nutty shit?

This is the dumb side of OCD. It will hijack your life and waste your time. But there is hope. You can put your obsessive tendencies to better use.

As an adult, I don't think of OCD as a disorder at all. It's more like a gift that you just need to control. Some days are better than others, and I still do some of the nutty shit, but not nearly the way I used to. Mostly, I channel all that nervous energy into worthwhile endeavors.

Instead of worrying about the precise order of boxes in the pantry, I learned to grab the bass and practice "The Number of the Beast." Even if I played it 666 times, I was still doing something worthwhile with my life. Instead of worrying about germs and hand sanitizer, I decided to work on my roundhouse kicks. Train your ass off and chase the demons away. That's what I'm talking about. Get shit done.

OCD gets me out of bed every day. Picture a leisurely Sunday morning with no obligations. What to do? Sleep in awhile longer? Make a cup of coffee; go out to your favorite patio chair; and enjoy the sunshine, trees, and singing birds?

Thanks anyway. For me, daylight begins to seep in, then consciousness—then the old noggin goes off like an alarm clock. Time to train. Ethyl Merman says so.

Get dressed. Kick. Punch. Block. Practice the form exactly twenty-five times. *Exactly*. It's the only way to quiet the brain. Let's go let's go let's go. This is the OCD fun train.

Not everybody has talent, but everyone has time. Everyone says, "Oh, I'd like to, but . . ." and "Oh, I'm so busy."

Bullshit.

What do you want to accomplish? If it matters enough, you have time—and if you have OCD, you have the ultimate planner, organizer, and time-management tool. You just have to use it for good instead of evil.

Now if you'll excuse me, I have to go wash my hands.

A NEW TWIST

I NEED to improve my flexibility. I've said that I've always been pretty pliant, and for a normal guy, that's true, but I'm not Korean flexible. I need work, and my success depends on it. I came to this realization the other day when I attempted a butterfly stretch. I could only get halfway down, and even then it felt like I split my groin in half. What the hell?

Then there's the matter of my hips. How do we generate power as martial artists? With the mind? No. I haven't met a telekinetic black belt. Yet. Do we generate power with the soul? Not unless you're James Brown. Power comes from the hips. This is one of the basic tenets of all martial arts and one of the first lessons we learn as white belts. A twist of the hips gives us power and snap. It's true if you're throwing roundhouse kicks in taekwondo or if you're throwing opponents in judo.

My hips are killing me, and this is far worse than any of my other aches and irritations. I just found out that my mom needs hip replacement, so every time I kick, I have that in the back of my mind. I may have major surgery to look forward to in twenty years. Unless I train hard. Then it will be fifteen.

On Thursday we sparred. It was my first time in weeks, and I did OK, but the tornado kicks are what got me. The tornado is a jumping, spinning kick, the sort of high-flying stuff taekwondo is famous for. It's not that hard to do, but I couldn't get it right because of my hips. I'm grinding them like an alchemist's mortar and pestle.

This makes me appreciate the way we rely on the hips for pretty much everything: walking, sitting, dancing, doing marriage pushups. When your hips hurt, your life hurts. I've tried Joint Juice, high-level yoga stretching, and elastic bands. Nothing has helped.

Then the other night . . . an epiphany. My wife asked me to dance.

Shelley and I were up way too late, goofy from a lack of sleep. We were flipping through TV channels when we found an old music show with Dick Clark. At first glance we thought it was *American Bandstand,* but it was actually *The Dick Clark Saturday Night Beechnut Show.* I've since looked it up. The airdate was August 6, 1960.

A young Dick Clark comes on to introduce the next act. He says, "This one is a gasser. This is a pretty frightening thing. It's sweeping the country, all over the place—hottest dance sensation in the last four years, a thing called the twist. Ladies and gentlemen, here's Chubby Checker."

Chubby comes out and performs an obvious lip-synch of "The Twist." All the goofy white kids in the audience clap on one and three.

Shelley enjoys music from the forties, fifties, and sixties. She's enamored of the clothing and the dances the kids used to do. She feels like she was born twenty years too late. She loves to dance and tries her best to drag me along. In twenty years of marriage I have yet to bite, but in twenty years of marriage she hasn't stopped trying. She pulled me off the couch, and I gave in. We were twistin' the night away.

We were having fun, dancing and laughing, and I thought, "Hey, this isn't so bad. My hips are moving all right."

Oh my God. That's it. The twist. The twist is the answer to my kicking problems.

I kept dancing the rest of that night and into the morning. Shelley was over it. She went to bed a half hour after my life-altering insight. When I finally turned in, my obliques were killing me, but I had worked out my calves, thighs, hips, and core—all because I followed Chubby's instructions. I've now added the twist to my daily exercise.

I'm a huge fan of surf music: Ventures, Huevos Rancheros, Los Straitjackets. It's perfect for twisting. I made a playlist of surf music, and now I twist fifteen minutes a day. I've noticed a considerable improvement in every kick. Roundhouses are better, spinning hook kicks are making heads spin, and my tornadoes are destroying trailers all over town. In sparring I even feel lighter on my feet and better able to anticipate an opponent's moves. Sparring is a dance after all.

It all makes sense. Bruce Lee was a Hong Kong cha-cha champion. He understood the importance of rhythm and pacing, and once your body comprehends this, watch out. If your sparring partner fights in four-four, and most do, then the ability to understand beats and rhythm will give you an upper hand. Bruce knew this. His dance experience helped him to identify and counter an opponent's moves.

As martial artists, we're always looking to improve our skills. We're after an edge, but we never know where or when we'll discover it. It can come from getting up at dawn to read *The Book of Five Rings*, or it might come from staying up all night to do the twist. You just have to be open to ideas from anywhere, anytime.

Want to become a master? Forget Musashi. Become a disciple of Chubby Checker.

I welcome your letters.

DON'T CALL ME A ROCK STAR

'VE JOKED that tens of people know me, but this time I'm serious: don't call me a rock star. I detest that term. It's just dirty. It assaults my ears and leaves me an aftertaste of bile and disgust.

For me, "rock star" conjures images of heroin girls and boys clad in leather, mascara running, snorting coke off a midget's ass. Their shows are filled with windmill picking, smashed guitars, naked breasts, and awful notes. The crowd roars with every electric squeal. They toss joints and bras and room keys on the smoke-filled stage.

"Good night, Bakersfield!"

Having just finished a hard night's "work," these "musicians" toss their "axes" to the roadies. All those quotation marks should tell you how I feel about this.

The majority of people who could fill out an application for rock star meet the following critical criteria. They are . . .

1. still relying on hair-care products, only now to conceal all that gray,

2. wearing shirts too small to cover their bulging guts,
3. thirty years past their prime,
4. hiring big-time producers to help them figure out how to be cool all these years later,
5. creating music that's a boring derivative of what they made in their twenties,
6. bitching about Spotify,
7. clueless about doing the thing that once came naturally to them, and
8. fake and far worse than their imitators.

OK, so maybe "rock star" isn't such a loaded term for you.

Rock stars, musicians . . . you might not see them the way I do, but whatever you call them, you'd have to admit they are not known for healthy living. Sure, Sting has his yoga, and John McLaughlin has his meditation. But I'll see your guru and raise you a Hendrix, a Moon, a Weiland, a Winehouse, a Presley, a Vicious, a Joplin, and a Bonham—plus one Prince and a King of Pop.

It sucks.

The stereotypes do come from somewhere. I'm not Jim Morrison, and no one will ever confuse me for him, but I would just like to say that you can live on a bus, play on big stages, and make good money doing it without living the clichés. I've been in this circus for more than two decades, and I've come up with a couple of ways to stay grounded: working and working out.

First, when I'm not in the studio or on the road with the band, I take straight jobs. For a lot of musicians, this is a terrifying prospect. They don't want to work a "real job" because they are . . . what? Busy being brilliant, I guess. The fear of going back to that gig at the Home Depot is just paralyzing. They have an image to uphold. What if people found out they aren't partying 24/7 and wiping their asses with hundred-dollar bills?

I've never lived that life, and I never wanted the image. Plus, I suck at sitting around. I've documented that pretty well by now. Another reason I work is that I'm a husband first. If music isn't paying the bills, then McDonald's will. My wife didn't ask me to marry her, you know. Guys who let their girls do all the work so they can "concentrate on music" make me puke. Get off your ass. Holding down a day job and playing music isn't hard. I've done it for twenty-five years. You can too.

Over the years, I've worked as a personal trainer, a truck driver, a barista, a music data coordinator, a coffee shop manager, a tech-support guy, and an assembler of tapes and CDs. This could be a dirty secret if I thought of myself as a rock star.

I have work and marriage to keep me grounded, and now I have martial arts. The Toadies are playing a run of shows, and this is my first time away since returning to taekwondo. I was just starting to make progress when the band got booked for work, and there's no way I'm going to take three months off.

Training on the road is interesting and challenging. Several times we have arrived in a city and found a beautiful, spacious park across from the venue. Picture the kind of place where you see nice older adults practicing tai chi. Fresh air, green grass, a pretty place to train—sounds great, doesn't it?

I don't work out there.

What would people think of me out in the open? Some spasmodic forty-one-year-old, tripping and killing himself as he attempted a roundhouse kick? That would really ruin the atmosphere.

I choose seclusion instead. I lock myself away in a sweaty, cramped backstage area, if I'm lucky to have even that. They usually smell of stale beer, tortilla chips, and the certainty that you're never going to get away from these kinds of places.

I really should go outside more. It's less depressing.

If you get creative while traveling, you can still find places to train: hotel rooms (after plenty of furniture moving), hotel gyms (unless someone else is there—God forbid), and even rooftops. Parking garages are also great. Very little light and loads of space.

From time to time I do see guys training in a park, going through forms or kicks. Regardless of whether their technique is right, they work out with no regard for who is around them. I'm pretty jealous of those guys. They seem focused, confident, and insulated from criticism. I hope to be like that someday. I want to go into any of the taegeuk in a public square without worrying whether people think I'm a nut. Because they will.

This from a guy who performs for a living? Strange, huh?

Training gives me a positive focus, a way to stay fit, and something constant when the scenery keeps changing. Training is also the only way to pacify Coach.

I suppose I should introduce you to Coach and Ivan, the two people who live in my head.

Coach is an asshole. He's my evil doppelgänger. Shouting insults is his sole means of communication. Success is his only concern, but he's never succeeded at anything himself. He's got a fat gut, a whistle, a clipboard, a trucker hat, and coach shorts—you know the kind. His gut hangs over them.

When I'm sore, he yells, "Put some dirt on it, sissy. Quit yer crying." When I'm getting tired, he yells, "Ray Nitschke will kick your sorry ass to kingdom come."

You can't tell him Nitschke is dead. There's no reasoning with Coach.

Coach is the sweating, screaming answer to Ivan. Ivan is my own self-image. He is timid and unsure. His legs are skinny, his face is riddled with acne, and he can barely do a push-up. The kid is forever on the verge of tears, but he never lets go of his emotions in a purge of crying. That would mean Coach wins.

No matter how bad Ivan wants to quit, Coach never lets up. No matter how Coach abuses Ivan, Ivan always takes it. They hate each other, but they need each other.

Ivan: I want to play bass.

Coach: Music is for girls. Get in there and work out, ya ballerina.

Ivan: I can't do this. I want some Cheetos.

Coach: Go ahead then. Get your Cheetos, quitter. You're the one who says you can do anything, like you're some goddamned Disney princess.

I told you Coach is an asshole.

I spend every day of my life trying to keep Coach happy. He never shuts the hell up. I do squats, calf raises, jumping jacks, and push-ups. I go through my entire taekwondo workout, just hoping to make Ivan a little tougher.

Shit. I probably should not have confessed all of this.

OK then. Let's summarize what I've written here:

1. I'm not a rock star, and I hate the term.
2. I think it's important to stay grounded.
3. I have two people living in my head.

IN MY SHED, WHERE I BELONG

B ATMAN HAD the Batcave and Dr. Strange his Sanctum Sanctorum. I have a shed. It doesn't have a secret tunnel accessible by fire pole, nor do I need to fly to the North Pole like Superman. I just go out behind the house.

We moved into our present home a year and a half ago. My wife and I were actually on the verge of giving up on the Panhandle. We'd been in Amarillo for fourteen years, and we thought maybe it was time to head back to the DFW. I imagined seeing Amarillo in my rearview mirror, and I was excited about what a new adventure might bring.

But the more we talked about it, the more we hesitated. Going back seemed like admitting defeat, like saying we couldn't handle small-town life so we had to return to party central. For years I had dreamed about leaving, and suddenly I didn't want to. We decided to investigate houses in Amarillo, just for shiggles. We'd waited fourteen years. We could wait a little longer until we were sure.

The search took time. Two weeks in, our realtor still wasn't getting it. We were clear about what we wanted—I thought we were clear, anyway—but she kept missing. We aren't the high-society Blairs, but we don't necessarily want a sagging roof and a hail-damaged Dodge Dart on blocks out front.

She insisted every house was *perfect* and *fabulous*. So positive. So damn perky. We should have fired her.

Our visits went something like this:

"This house has a roof."

Well, that's a pro.

"I just love the wallpaper. It's so *Little House on the Prairie*."

Con.

"This is the master bedroom. The carpet is a vintage 1973 *Houses of the Holy* orange."

Hmm. Well . . . con. I'd be more inclined if it were *Physical Graffiti* brown.

"Look, guys. Your new neighbors love the Confederate flag."

Con.

"You have easy access to the firing range across the road."

Eventually, my wife took over the search, and we just made Perky book the viewings. That led us here. It's perfect: a huge kitchen, hardwood floors, an open view, a park across the street. And it's in a secluded area. A lot of people around here don't know this part of town exists. That's a pro all the way.

I liked the house from the start, but for me the clincher came when we checked out the backyard. There it was: my fortress of solitude, my clubhouse—No Dames Allowed.

To the casual observer, this may be just a 20 x 50 corrugated metal shed. To me it is a private dojang. As a kid I always loved the idea of having a clubhouse and a secret knock, and this place satisfies that adolescent need. My shed is mine and mine alone. You won't find a woman's touch or lavender-scented anything.

Now, I know what you're thinking, so let me stop you right there. This is definitely not a "man cave." I've heard about man caves—although only women use the term. That is not what we have here. Yes, it's detached from the house. Yes, it's dedicated to nerdy martial arts activities. And sure, it does smell like a dead rat in a gym sock. But from what I can gather, a man cave is a place where you get drunk and watch NASCAR. You turn on the Cowboys; get lit; argue with your best friend about who's better, Troy or Romo; tell him to shit and fall back in it; and then end the night with a black eye.

I'm not interested in any of that. This is where I practice my skills, or lack thereof—and work off the wife's homemade Snickers fudge. This is my happy place.

Granted, when I first cracked the door, it took a little imagination to see that. The previous owner had left behind a heap of scrap metal and a liquor still. The whole place smelled of weed, even after sitting vacant for months.

I imagine the guy alone in his shop o' wonders, stoned out of his mind, trying to piece together metal and screws to build some Frankensteinian masterpiece. Of course he's cranking Van Hagar on the hi-fi. He slips, saws off a few fingers, and the memory haunts him, so he decides to sell the house and let some other idiot have it.

I am that idiot.

I hauled out the debris, swept, and vacuumed. I aired out the place, and then I laid carpet so I could work out in bare feet without fear of splinters. That was a major improvement, even though I have caught a loose carpet staple once or twice.

"Hiyah!"

"OHsonofaBITCH."

The shelves remain, but the old gardening tools, hammers, and nails are gone, replaced with books by Benny the Jet, Bill "Superfoot" Wallace, and other guys with names like Ironface or

Dongfist. Or is it Ironfist and Dongface? Either way they sound like my comic-book heroes of old.

Then there's the training equipment. I need to make impact with an actual target because kicking the air sucks. Oh, it looks fantastic on film with a classroom full of people kicking in unison, every breath in time like the woodwind section in an orchestra, but space won't absorb a blow. There is no worse strike than the one that does not connect. A lot of martial artists wind up needing elbow and knee surgery because of repeated striking at the air.

I've outfitted the shed with six different kicking bags. I have a BOB, which is a full-body target with a neck and face—a gift from my wife. I use that to practice headshots, side kicks, and punches. There's a Wavemaster that has decreased padding due to all the abuse. Now when I kick it, my foot hits the hard plastic center. Kind of like a Tootsie Roll Pop, it takes *whuhun, tahoo, tharee* licks to get to the center. I've affixed other pads to the wall at various heights for tornado and axe kicks. I have to watch out for the overhanging light. I've hit my head, arms, and legs on it. I'm working on precision.

Other treasures of the shed: knee braces; elbow braces; wraparound ankle weights; boxing gloves; dumbbells; broken kicking mitts; and a dumb, rusted sword. Then there's my vintage *A Force of One* poster.

Remember that movie? It really is among the finest in the oeuvre of Chuck Norris. I can just hear the voiceover guy now: *"A Force of One*: It starts with a routine search. It ends with a trail of bodies." If you haven't seen it, check it out. It's no *Lone Wolf McQuade*, but you know . . . Chuck Norris.

In the summer the shed is hotter than a monkey's asshole. There is no AC. I raise every window and turn on the fan, which just blows in hot air and wasps. They buzz my head like I'm King Kong and they're biplanes and I'm climbing the Empire State Building and I'm just trying to get away but no one understands me and the planes are closing in and . . .

Sorry. Geeking out again.

I use TKD shoes to splatter flying insects. I don't actually wear TKD shoes. They are just overpriced flyswatters. One day I was practicing Koryo, a black belt form, when a brave hornet dove for my face. I dodged him but ended up tearing the *A Force of One* poster. Sad but true. That bastard got his due when I caught up with him.

I do a ton of repetitions on a typical day in the shed, so I begin by setting a metronome to a hundred BPM. I blow through fifty kicks (each side, each kick) and a hundred punches followed by blocks and then form work—all with the constant three-four *ding*-ding-ding of the metronome. Hey, I'm a bassist. A lead singer would never train to a click track.

I kick and punch in time, hollering and sweating. My neighbor rolls his Harley out of the garage and revs it. He doesn't go anywhere. He just revs it again and again, and I think, "Just ride it, man, far away from here." Meanwhile the drummer a few houses down practices his Slipknot songs. His tempo is deplorable. These distractions are tough on an ADD guy.

Damn it, Doni. Must focus.

Moving into a new place is never simple. It's a painful process. As a kid my family was always on the move, like New Age seekers, like white-trash gypsies. Either our place sucked and my mom hated it or the rent was due and we had to get out. I got good at moving furniture at three in the morning. I was too young to be embarrassed about it. And once I was old enough to know better, I just didn't care what the neighbors said. My parents had their reasons for moving constantly, but how could Zach and I argue with them? They hadn't bought new clothes in ten years because their priority was to keep us in new shit.

All these years later, I can never fully settle and relax until the boxes are gone, the clothes are on hangers, and our Chuck Norris posters are on the wall. I find serenity in knowing everything is where it needs to be.

That's how I feel in the shed. When I'm working out here, every-thing's OK. Good days, bad days, angry days. Even with the heat, the wasps, the Harley, and the tempo-deficient Slipknot perfor-mance. This is home.

HAVE YOU EVER HAD TO USE IT?

W HEN PEOPLE who aren't involved in martial arts find out you are training in a particular style, there's one question they can't resist asking: "Have you ever had to use it?" They picture scenes from *Kung Fu Hustle*, and I guess they want you to regale them with inflated stories of the brawls you've been in, trashing assholes ten at a time.

"Have you ever had to use it?" To someone who has been training for a while, it's a funny question, and it means something very different. You use it every day, in your mental and physical balance, in the way you see the world. You use it to stay fit and flexible. And yes, if you're in a bad neighborhood after dark and some shady character is eyeing you, you do feel more confident about the situation. But your time in martial arts is mostly peaceful. It's not some bust-'em-up scene with fists flying and bottles smashing.

Except on those rare occasions when it is some bust-'em-up scene with fists flying and bottles smashing.

This happened a few years back. It was before I started training with the grandmaster, but I had been dabbling with some kung fu on my own. Shelley and I went to Ft. Collins, Colorado, to visit Zach. He was at a studio there, making a record with Rise Against. We all went out for a night on the town, doing as much partying as a straight-edge group can do. We were hanging out at a club called Surfside 7, drinking lots of Cokes with lots of ice, and talking shit.

Then a drunk-edge couple in the crowd caught our attention. The guy got into an altercation with his lady. It was violent. It was ugly. It was also none of my goddamn business, as Shelley informed me. When my partner of over two decades makes sense, I ignore her, of course.

I stepped between the couple. I figured I could put some distance between them. Then she could get away. Maybe she'd call the police. She'd be free of this dickhead, start a new life, perhaps finish that novel she'd always dreamed of writing.

Instead she bashed me in the head.

Then he punched me in the face.

My damn brother was standing off to the side, bored. He was used to the experience. *Hot. There's Doni, sticking his nose into some shit again.* If he had been Iron Fist to my Power Man, this whole thing would have turned out better.

I sure as hell wasn't going to fight a girl, so the guy got double the action, but the next morning I woke up with a black eye, broken glasses, and a pissed-off wife.

Does Zorro deal with this too? They never show you that scene.

*   *   *

"Don't take shit from anybody."

This was my parents' advice to my brother and me through our entire lives. Not "Do well in school so you can get into college and get a job." Not "Find a nice girl to settle down with." Not even

"Brush your teeth between meals." It was more important that we never back down from anyone. Anyone.

I don't mean to cast the blame, but I do think this is why I was always a little prick. I admit it. When people wanted to screw with me, I just couldn't step away. Some part of me wanted to make the situation worse. Even if I got my head kicked in, I didn't back down, so in some weird way, I still won.

When someone started shit, I heard my old man's mantra ringing in my head. Then I pushed back. Then cue the redness in my brain and voilà: a black eye the next morning. If I had known a martial art back then, I would have most definitely "used it."

Kids compete and fight for status all the time. It's just a fact of growing up. That's why it's the job of every big brother to prepare his little brother for this reality. Stated another way, pissing off your little brother is a timeless tradition.

This looks peaceful enough, but I'm actually employing psychological warfare against Zach.

I'm eighteen months older than Zach, and when we were growing up, he hated when I touched him. Just a tap and he'd scream and freak the fuck out. It was awesome. It was all I could do, just prod at him all day long. I'd never had that kind of power over anyone. I couldn't stop using it. Poke at the toddler and he goes off. Bump the six-year-old and it's warheads. I loved it, and I didn't care when it got me into trouble with my mom.

My brother was my plaything. Here's another favorite gag of mine that I still do to this day. I wait until Zach is taking a sip of a drink. As soon as it's in his mouth, I spring, saying something dumb or making a really horrible face—anything to make him laugh and do a spit take. When we were kids, I did this in the car, and it usually went all over the back of our dad's seat. Zach had to sit behind him so my mom could keep an eye on him. I don't remember much about our cars, just the backs of my old man's seats. They were always messed up and dirty with sprayed Coke, water, food—you name it. As soon as Zach would play Old Faithful, I'd be the one getting in trouble, not him. It makes sense: you don't blame the gun for shooting; you blame the guy who pulled the trigger.

I have a picture of my brother and me when we were one and three years old. We're in a photo studio, both sitting on a blanket. I look like a girl because my hippie dad refused to cut my hair. Zach and I are wearing matching Mouseketeers shirts. But what really stands out is the look of glee on my face. It's not because the photographer said "cheese" and squeaked a rubber ducky at me. It's because I have my hand on my brother's arm and the camera flash caught his face as he was about to go nuclear.

It's the little things.

I recently asked my mom about this. She said, "You were drunk on power." It's true. I have a lot of photos that show the same scenario.

As we got older, I discovered Zach had also listened to my folks' advice about taking shit from no one. He embraced that

Don't touch the baby. He will explode.

Zach goes ballistic in three, two . . . .

philosophy, especially when it came to me. He didn't just scream anymore. He answered with punches and kicks. The kid was no longer my plaything, and that was disappointing, but I had to respect it. Like it or not, punches and kicks tend to get respect. We still scrapped, but it wasn't as much fun when I knew Zach would no longer allow the torment to go unanswered.

Then we started at Piner Junior High. Zach got into altercations with the "ropers" (the cowboy kids) and with the African American kids, who made up the majority of the class. They saw a weird little skinny white kid wearing floods, high-water pants. They saw his tangled-up hair and thought, "I gotta screw with this guy." And they did, a lot.

When I saw him in a showdown with the other kids, I realized I had a new rule: no one gets to hit my brother but me. Period. We were a package deal. We were longhaired metal geeks, and I think our mom sprayed us with pussy repellant at night in our sleep. No one thought we were cool. We had to stick together.

I was nuts and couldn't have cared less that I was inches away from a hospital bed. I fought back so many times that they eventually left me alone, figuring it wasn't worth the trip to the principal's office. And over time, I gained their respect because, true to my old man's instruction, I didn't take shit. From anyone.

Zach became braver when I was around. He knew I had his back, and he was more outspoken because of it. As soon as the shit went down, he could trust his 36 Crazyfists brother to start swinging in an orgy of nerd rage. *Someone* was getting punched. It could have been a guy on my team for all I knew. I just threw punches; it wasn't up to me where they landed.

I dreamed of having Chuck Norris's patented spin kick. He could turn in a flash and lay you flat, and I wanted that power over my enemies. I also wanted to flick ninja stars by the dozen. In every scenario I dreamed of using my impeccable kicking and flicking skills to defend my latest crush—a girl who most definitely had no idea of my existence.

"You were scared of my kicks," I'd imagine telling my nemesis, "but just wait until I bring out my nunchaku. Yeah, that's what I thought."

No wonder I got my ass kicked.

Staff Photo by David Arndt

New generation of authors

Piner Middle School student Doni Blair reads "No Baths For Peter," a book he wrote, to children at Jack and Jen Day Care Center. Doni and other students in Diane Clark's reading and writing enrichment course — "Getting Into Books" — wrote, illustrated and bound the books, then presented them to the pre-schoolers. Later, the young writers had an "author's tea" to celebrate the publication of their works. 12-5-84

A clipping from the *Sherman Democrat*, December 5, 1984. I found time between fights to indulge my literary pretentions. In this shot, I'm reading a bunch of preschoolers an original story with the dubious name "No Baths for Peter." I don't know how I got that one past the censors.

These fantasies occupied so much of my youth, but when I actually did defend myself like my heroes, it would make my stomach turn. Violent confrontations look so compelling in the movies, but in real life they just make you feel sick and jittery.

After Piner Junior High, I entered high school with the same guys who used to pick on me. An interesting thing happened: when some meathead started shit, before I could respond, my old tormentors would rush beside me and quash the whole thing. I'd earned their respect, and they looked out for me.

So let's summarize. I was an unpopular kid who got picked on and lost too many fights. I never backed down from anyone. And now I'm training in taekwondo. Sounds like a mix for disaster, right?

Actually, this is why I need martial arts in my life. I have to restrain my inner asshole and become someone worthy of learning these skills. Maybe someday I'll even back down from a confrontation. Maybe.

I can't say I am totally reformed, but since I've returned to taekwondo, I haven't had any trouble with anyone. Maybe I have more discipline now. Maybe the douchebags pick up a feeling from me, and they don't want to test me. Or maybe I just avoid confrontation because I'm too damn tired from training in the shed in triple-digit heat.

ON PRACTICING

MARTIAL ARTS and music are deep in our human DNA. People fought and protected themselves way before they wrote books about it, and they made interesting sounds way before they recorded them. The full details are more than anyone could ever know. Even if you just consider a little slice of each discipline—say martial books and rock records—we're still talking about a lifetime of study.

If I'm going to be serious about any art, I want to know its history, evolution, and techniques. I want to know the stories and the people who lived them. Where martial arts and rock and roll are concerned, those people are legendary. We're talking Bruce Lee and Elvis, Chuck Norris and Paul McCartney, Jean Claude Van Damme and David Bowie. It might look a little funny to see those names run together like that, but to me it makes perfect sense.

And once you know about those guys, you go a little deeper: Jeffrey Falcon and Robin Trower, Sho Kosugi and Paul Weller, Iko Uwais and Phil Lynott.

If you take up music to get chicks and make money, you will be disappointed. If you take up taekwondo to kick stuff and yell *hiyah*, you'll be disappointed again. You'll probably find the real work boring and frustrating. You have to come to terms with what it takes to get it right. Yes, it takes hard work and dedication—all that puritanical stuff—but more than anything else, it takes time. Lots of time.

When we see amazing martial artists, they move so fast that we can barely pick up what they're doing. You know what else we can't see? The years of slow, methodical training it took to get there. We're talking focus and exhaustive repetition but also the creativity and endurance to get through times when practice feels uninspired and tedious.

This is what master martial artists have in common with master musicians. I don't think of myself as either one, but I have practiced an instrument for most of my life, so I can't help but see that connection.

When Zach was a kid, he took guitar lessons from a guy named Phil. Everyone in town said Phil was the best. I think this was based on his ability to teach kids the shit their parents wanted to hear—shit like the Eagles and, God help me, Bob Seger.

"Well, I wasn't crazy about little Bubba taking up guitar, but do you know the other day I heard him playing 'Peaceful Easy Feeling'? Wow."

"Oh yeah? Our little Billy Bob is playing 'Old Time Rock and Roll.' He's a musical genius."

My brother lasted five lessons and learned enough to teach himself some songs. Then he showed me the basics. Fret here. Pluck there. Now you're making music. We jammed together, and my dad pulled the plug on Zach's lessons. Why pay some schmuck if we could learn for ourselves? We had to find our own path.

I am a natural lefty, but my folks got me a right-handed bass. This was Christmas of 1985. My dad had the guy at the guitar shop string it upside down. Paul McCartney did this with his first guitars, and my bass even looked like Paul's Hofner. I fumbled with scales and battled the stupid metronome my dad bought us. *Click, click, click* . . . it was Chinese water torture. I couldn't play on time. I couldn't even coax a decent sound out of my instrument.

Pops didn't want me to give up, so he said inspiring stuff like, "I paid a lot of goddamn money for that thing. Learn how to play it."

In desperation I switched the strings around and tried playing righty again. That was the answer. I taught myself the Beatles' "Day Tripper" and Rush's "New World Man" in an afternoon. I had struggled for a couple of weeks, doubting myself, and suddenly I got it. I've been playing right handed ever since.

After that breakthrough, practice was no longer a chore. I sat down in front of the stereo with my bass every day, and I loved it. I had no amp, so I leaned in to hear the instrument better. I'd pluck my way through songs one note at a time. Hear Paul play it, match the pitch, and then pluck hard enough to produce a sound. My right hand got stronger not from technical exercises but from learning pretty much every Iron Maiden song I'd ever heard. It took a while to nail them at tempo, but once I did, I imagined I'd stumbled upon a new kind of alchemy: turning patience into music.

Before that, I'd never actually sat down and focused on anything. My schoolwork was easy, so I didn't study. I couldn't study anyway. My ADD brain would take over, and I'd wander off in search of something more exciting than solving for X. But music showed me I could actually sit and focus for hours, working through every detail. I wasn't a defective hyperactive kid after all; I could learn songs, and those songs made me someone else.

Practice became my religion—and my religion was badass. The apostles were Geezer Butler of Black Sabbath, Jaco Pastorius, and Geddy Lee of Rush. Our hymns included "Electric Funeral," "Continuum," and "Working Man."

I can't even tell you all the hours I spent analyzing Geddy's playing. "Lead bass" sounds like a bad idea, but in his hands, it's brilliant. He weaves melodically through the song and still stays right in Neil Peart's pocket. It's mind blowing, like a rocket ride to Cygnus X-1.

Listen to the live version of "The Trees" from *Exit, Stage Left*. Listen to "Digital Man" from *Signals*. Then consider that these songs came out in 1981 and 1982, when the biggest hits were "Bette Davis Eyes," by Kim Carnes, and "Physical," by Olivia Newton John.

Then there's Karl Alvarez from Descendents. He can dazzle on the fretboard, but he can also lay back and groove like "Duck" Dunn. Karl's sense of harmony is nothing short of extraterrestrial. He's the only punk-rock bassist who can put jazz extensions and inversions in a simple three-minute punk song, all without anyone knowing—or understanding what the fuck just happened. Insane.

If you go only as deep as Wikipedia on Karl, you will read about some records he played on. You'll see that "Australian punk band Frenzal Rhomb wrote a song about Karl, on their 2011 album, *Smoko at the Pet Food Factory*." These are factoids. You need to experience the man's work.

My formative years as a musician are long gone, but I'm still an obsessive student. I knew that would follow me to the dojang. I can't go there twice a week and leave it at that, so when the training day is done, I turn to books, videos, and films. Martial arts have a deep tradition of technique, philosophy, history, and myth. My martial library is piling up. I couldn't list it all, but here are a few favorites I keep in reach.

There's the technical side: Wong's *Dynamic Strength*, Lee's *The Art of Expressing the Human Body*, and Huang's excellent DVD *The Kick Coach*.

The philosophical side: Musashi's *The Book of Five Rings*, Levine's *Dharma Punx*, and the Dalai Lama's *How to Practice: The Way to a Meaningful Life*.

There's the nonfiction side: Mailer's *The Fight*, Sheridan's *A Fighter's Heart*, and St-Pierre's *The Way of the Fight*.

And the fiction side: Donohue's *Deshi*, Murray and Sapir's Destroyer series, and Barker's Ninja Master series, which is super corny but oh so good.

A discussion of killer martial arts films would require another book, but a few favorites include *The Raid: Redemption*, *Iron Monkey*, and *Ip Man*.

Geeking out over these titles reminds me of the way I geeked out over bass as a kid. You dive into a world of ideas. Some you can experiment with during the next session, and others are more abstract, but they seep in one way or another and make you keep up the pursuit.

What else do music and martial arts have in common? Rhythm. Timing. Motion. Whether you're sparring or in a street fight, you need to understand the dance. Figure out your opponent's tempo, and you'll know where his feet will land. It's like having a sixth sense.

When you start playing music as a kid, you just go for it. You don't really listen to your bandmates; it's tough enough to get your own parts right. You may be surprised when your lines clash with theirs.

When you're in your first sparring matches, you have an agenda. You know what you want to do, but you're not really sure how that will fit with the other guy's agenda. You may be surprised to learn that he doesn't have to let you hit him.

Experienced musicians are relaxed. They listen and understand your timing and your feel. These are the guys you want to play with. Experienced fighters are relaxed too. They watch and understand your timing and your feel. These are not the guys you want to play with.

When I spar, I tend to play different songs in my head. That way it's difficult to get a read on my rhythm. One minute I think of "Stepping Out," by Joe Jackson. Then I flip my internal radio to "Ain't This the Life," by Oingo Boingo. My eighteen-year-old opponents have never even heard these songs. They will never figure me out.

I think these reflections on practice sound positive enough—weird maybe, but positive. Well, I'd be remiss if I didn't mention that practice can also have a dark side. You can become a slave to it. You can hurt yourself overtraining. You can lose all perspective and sacrifice the friends and relationships you once valued. I know a little about this.

I've never just picked up a new skill. I'm not one to get it on the first crack. Part of the reason is that I make everything harder and more complicated than it has to be. This infuriates nearly everyone I know, but I'm certain if something is too easy, then it's wrong. Even if the task is simple, I'll find a way to confuse it.

If you need to go through a brick wall, what do you do? Get a wrecking ball, right? I prefer to beat my head against the bricks until I've dislodged every last one.

That's the dark side.

The good thing about committing to a lifetime of practice is that you never stop. The bad thing is that you never stop. Proceed with caution.

I know I'm going to sound like a cranky old guy here, but I don't care. People want everything fast and easy: information, entertainment, relationships, meals. The faster and easier they come, the more we think we can take on. Music is the one subject I know well in my life, and that's because of relentless, ridiculous work. As I make progress in martial arts, I recognize that the path is the same. I don't want a shortcut. I wouldn't know what to do with myself.

When I was a kid, I practiced like mad because I wanted to be the best, whatever that meant. At some point I realized I wouldn't become Mozart—or Joey Ramone. As an adult starting again in martial arts, I want to be good. No, I want to be great. But more than anything, I just want to understand. I want to get it. I'm not competing with anyone anymore, even when I'm sparring.

Why did my goals change? Eventually you realize you'll never have the fastest pick or the fastest kicks. That doesn't negate all the hard work. It actually frees you to become an artist in your own right. This happens when you learn the fundamentals and study the history—and then give yourself permission to find your own path.

WHEEL OF TORTURE

Strength or flexibility? Flexibility or strength? This debate comes up in many athletic pursuits. You need to be flexible and strong, but those two needs often compete with each other. If you build a lot of muscle, it can be tough to stay loose.

You don't need a ton of muscle in martial arts, and you don't want bulk, but you must be pliant. If you can't bend, you'll crack like a wishbone. Taekwondo in particular is known for high-flying, groin-splitting kicks. Any schlub off the street can kick you in the gut; a practitioner of taekwondo, and a black belt in particular, needs the ability to kick the hat off someone's head. Or just kick someone's head off. That's the rule, and I take it to heart. If I throw a side kick, that son of a bitch better be pointed at the sky.

I'm pretty flexible, especially for a guy in his forties, but I'm not Korean flexible. I've needed to push, to stretch more and stretch deeper to get the results I'm after. I've made progress, but now I feel my limitations again. I do a ton of squats and calf raises, and

I look as if I could kick through a wall—at least a modest piece of sheetrock—but size can hinder elasticity. I need a way to go deeper.

This is a good time to talk about equipment.

If you want to play rock and roll, you'll need to buy a lot of expensive gear. It will cost you hundreds to become a hobbyist, and if you become a professional, you'll probably spend tens of thousands. Through the years, people will try to sell you a lot of dumb shit you don't need. Think of it this way: a bass, an amp, and a tuner are essential; bass tremolo, guitar-string lubricant, and a pick pocket that attaches to your instrument are not.

Want to get better? Put your credit card away and go practice.

This is something I love about martial arts. Instruction is the only real financial expense—well, that and the occasional medical bill. You pay for knowledge and invest your time. The rest is about hard work, which is not for sale. You can work out in shorts and bare feet. You can become a master in the third world, training with sticks and tree stumps. You can be a political prisoner in solitary confinement, but if you know what you're doing, you can keep your skills sharp.

Of course, martial artists can and do buy plenty of other equipment, some expensive, some helpful, some silly and pointless. You can spend your money on uniforms, gloves, pads, headgear, special shoes, focus mitts, books, videos, and weapons of every sort. You can buy a foam floor, a mat, a kicking shield, a speed bag, a hanging bag, a standing bag, a double-end bag, an uppercut bag, a grappling dummy, a Wing Chun dummy, and a dummy head.

But wait! Order now, and we'll also throw in a punch sensor, a karate dinner plate, a personalized belt-display rack, and a Sammo Hung signature jockstrap.

I made up the last one. I think.

I don't have all of that stuff. But I have a lot of it. But I don't need it. I'm not a hypocrite or anything. I can quit anytime I want.

Because my flexibility needs some work, I made another little purchase. I bought a pulley system designed to tear martial artists apart at the seams. You can just call it a stretcher because you'll get wheeled off in one when you finish.

The design is simple. You attach a metal ring to the ceiling. A cable runs through the ring, and at the end of that cable is what I can describe only as a noose. Put your foot in the noose, and give the cable a yank. Or you might prefer to ease into it.

You can use this system to improve flexibility or extract confessions. It resembles a torture device used during the Spanish Inquisition. It feels like one too. If you enjoy the sensation of your legs being pulled off your hips, you will love it. Bruce Lee used a similar system during the sixties. This may come as some surprise, but I am not Bruce Lee.

I had no problem plunking down fifteen bucks on this pulley system. A few alternatives include daily yoga, which is free; a belt from Walmart, which is about three dollars; or a seated stretching machine, which costs a couple of hundred bucks.

That last option is especially effective—and especially ridiculous. In the middle it has what looks like a steering wheel. You sit in the saddle, start cranking the wheel of torture, and hilarity ensues.

As I said, though, it does work, and I need results. It's tempting, but I don't have the floor space for it in the shed. And anyway, where the hell would I find that money? I'm already selling an amp just to pay for this year's taekwondo classes. I guess I could turn a few tricks on the mean streets of Amarillo. There's always the TA off I-40—and if I took the pulley stretcher, it might be good for business.

*   *   *

Update: OK. I, uh, broke down and bought the seated stretching machine, steering wheel and all. It required no acts of prostitution, but it did cost me 250 bones.

Don't judge me. And don't trust me with national security secrets.

Yes, it was a lot of money, and yeah, I don't really have space for it in the shed, so I put it in the living room and use it while watching *American Ninja Warrior*. We all have our methods. I can still quit anytime I want.

I spent another wad of cash on my martial habit, and I didn't expect that, but then nobody expects the Spanish Inquisition.

"STRATEGERY"

MY TAEKWONDO classmates used to beat the piss out of me. My strategy involved letting them wear themselves down, which isn't a bad idea until you consider that they were wearing themselves down by beating the piss out of me. I got in a few kicks, but for the most part I was a heavy bag with legs.

I decided to take a different look at sparring. I've been studying boxing's evasive techniques, and I've changed my focus from delivering strikes to just getting out of the way. I use a little ducking and a little footwork. Simple enough, but something remarkable has happened: I'm not a human *makiwara* anymore.

I spar with teenagers whose sole mission is to beat up a forty-something dude—and let's be honest about that: I am standing in for every parent, coach, teacher, principal, and cop who's ever told them what to do. I am a human voodoo doll, taking beatings on behalf of authority figures everywhere. But the dynamic is changing. Oh, these kids are still younger and faster, and they always will be, but now they miss a lot more. Evasion is the answer. It's a revelation for all of us.

Another key to a successful bout is muting your doubts and fears. You can strategize all you want beforehand, but during the match, you have to quiet the mind. That's tough to do when someone's trying to hit you, but the exchanges happen too fast to reason through every move. It's a cliché to say "Be in the moment," but that's the deal. Forget about the previous injuries. Ignore the voice that says, "This kid pummeled you last time, and he's about to do it again." You just have to concentrate on the task at hand.

I'm not saying I can always dial in that sort of focus, but there are times that I feel it, and if you get a glimpse of it, you know which way to go.

I used to dread sparring. It's still not my favorite part of training, but I do see how important it is. We can train night and day, snapping kicks and punches in the air, but the air doesn't fight back. The only way to know where you stand is to test your skills against others.

My sparring matches and research into boxing have also given me a new perspective on what professional fighters do. It's like taking a course on music appreciation: you might still prefer the Misfits, but after studying Beethoven, you'll never listen to him the same again.

Well, I guess it's like that, except people don't hit you in the head when you're in class, dozing off in MU 111, so that's where the analogy breaks down.

I realize I'm an aficionado of combat sports. That's it. I have no pretentions about my abilities. I can train and study all I want, and I can get better, but none of that will ever compare to what a career fighter goes through.

Not long ago, a friend and I were watching a fight featuring the Dutch kickboxer Nieky Holzken. The match started, and the fighters were feeling one another out. My buddy turned to me and said, "You know, I'm just as good as anyone in that ring."

He was serious.

"The only thing keeping me from it," he added, "is a bad back."

Right.

Or a bad hip. Or an ACL injury. Or a day job. Or a wife or girlfriend who says you're not allowed to fight. Whatever the excuse, there's always an excuse. I've heard it so many times from so many different guys that I can finish their sentences for them. These dudes are master pugilists—and their own hype men. They spit an unbroken stream of superlatives to describe their own badass abilities. They do everything but fight.

Here's my question: what the hell are they thinking? We are watching professional fighters, guys who have been in gyms and rings since they were little kids. They train for eight hours a day, running hills, jumping rope, hitting bags, and sparring. They have nutritionists and doctors, trainers and sparring partners, and all those guys are professionals too.

You work at Office Depot, and you're sitting on my couch. That's the difference between an amateur and a professional.

Professional fighters take on other professional fighters—guys who work just as hard—and they do it in front of thousands of people, a camera crew, and millions of people at home. Meanwhile, some everyday dude in Amarillo says he could be a champion. Give me a fucking break.

That's like walking into Axes Я Us and having a salesman tell you how he could be Steve Vai if he wanted to. Right. So you almost wrote *Passion and Warfare*, but you decided to work retail for minimum wage in Laredo instead? A managerial spot will be open in a couple of years.

Do you suppose Steve Vai ever says, "You know, I could work at Axes Я Us El Paso if I really wanted to"? What separates him from them is beyond measure.

Look, I love martial arts, and I train my ass off. I've also been in fights in real life. Big damn deal. All of that would amount to nothing if I stepped into the ring to face Nieky Holzken or any of his peers. There would be no way to quiet those doubts and fears. The only strategy to get me through would have to involve a sniper.

I'd get killed. Murdered. Dismembered, stuffed in plastic bags, and buried in the desert.

If I were lucky, I'd get out of there with just a good maiming. Then I'd send Nieky a thank-you card from my hospital bed.

That's the difference between an amateur and a professional.

'CAUSE A GUY READS COMICS
HE CAN'T START SOME SHIT?

STILL want to be a superhero.

I'm a comic-book nerd of the first order, and I have been since I was five. This is my father's doing. He loved comics and wanted to share them with my brother and me. Every night without fail he would read them to us before bed.

Some kids get bedtime tales of gnomes and fairies. Some get Bible lessons, God help them. Zach and I got stories of how Bruce Wayne's parents were murdered and why he turned into Batman. Or why the Master of Kung Fu's father wanted to kill him.

In the world of comics, these origin stories describe how regular people turned into the characters we know and love. This stuff has always fascinated me. Take an orphan, toss him into a laboratory, knock over a Bunsen burner, and *poof*: a superhero is born.

A good ass-kicking is a prerequisite for a comic book, as is some kind of showdown between good and evil. Martial arts can help with both. As a kid, many of my favorite comic characters were martial artists: Shang Chi, Iron Fist, and the Karate Kid. Not *that* Karate Kid. This one was a member of the Legion of Super-Heroes when Ralph Macchio was just a boy.

I had a head full of these tales by the time I was seven. Every night my pops would select whatever story fit his mood: *Jonah Hex, Dr. Strange, Power Man and Iron Fist.* Stan Lee and Marv Wolfman fit my definition of literary giants. I could still make a case for that.

At some point, though, Zach and I asked my dad to stop reading us comics. We thought we had outgrown it. The bedtime readings came to an end, and, although we didn't admit it, we missed his stories. I'm sure he did too. Growing up complicates everything.

I still have crime fighters on the brain. Every kid dreams of saving the world, or at least the city, but most of them get over it by the time they're in their forties. Since my return to martial arts, I feel that calling once again. My inner superhero is in the closet, and he needs to get into his tights, come out, and be fabulous and free.

Sorry.

How do you create a superhero? First I need a cool origin. OK, let's see. I was born in a mystical faraway city called Sherman, Texas.

No. Start again.

I was just your average, mild-mannered bassist/barista. One night I was the last person at the coffee shop. I locked up and walked outside, and that was when I heard someone calling for help. I ran to the corner and looked down the alley. Two guys were attacking a woman. They had taken her purse and ripped her shirt, and it looked like they were about to do something much worse to her.

She saw me and screamed again for help. Time seemed to slow down. I looked down the street, but no one else was around. What could I do? The extent of my superpowers included hollering, "I have a no-foam latte for Brenda."

"Well," I thought, "here goes." I ran down the alley, straight into the fray. The bad guys left the woman alone but proceeded to beat the crap out of me.

A few nights later I was in the coffee shop again. I still had a black eye. It was a slow night, so I was reading an old *Master of Kung Fu* comic to pass the time. Storm clouds rolled across the plains, and rain began to fall on Amarillo. The last customers headed out. The storm became more intense. I was ten minutes from locking up for the night.

That's when it happened: a bolt of lightning struck the roof, traveled down the building, and zapped me through the Cecilware Venezia II espresso machine.

A superhero was born.

I became . . . the Amarillo Avenger, with the power to . . . play bass. *Slap! Pop!* And make skinny hazelnut soy cappuccinos. *Trickle-trickle-trickle!* And kick ass. *Pow! Bap!*

That's all I have so far. I still have to figure out some details. For example, what kind of costume do I wear?

Standard-issue tights. No cape because, well, give me a break. I'll have a ninja hood and the whole outfit will be bright yellow. The Amarillo Avenger can't very well show up in red.

What do I drive?

The Batmobile is cool and all, but can you imagine the payments on that thing? I'll get around on a Genuine Scooter. It's great on gas. It's black, so with my yellow costume, I'll look like a bumblebee in traffic. The Genuine pushes speeds of forty miles an hour—sixty downhill. Amarillo is flatter than Taylor Swift, but as long as the bad guys don't go too fast, I can keep them in my sights.

How do I watch out for crime?

Spiderman swings from tall buildings. He tucks himself against the sides of skyscrapers to observe wrongdoings. We have one— I'm serious—*one* tall building in Amarillo. It's Chase Tower, thirty-one stories high. I guess I could just swing around that nonstop.

Who are those bad guys?

Our crime mainly concerns meth labs. They are in trailers on farmland outside of town, and they have the tendency to blow up. That's a real nuisance, especially if you're just getting to the fast part at the end of "Free Bird."

My main nemeses will be MethHead and Alabama Man. One will be fast but only for five minutes at a time. The other will carry a butterfly knife and brass knuckles while draped in a Confederate flag.

Shit. I don't think this is going to make much of a comic. It's just got one storyline, and if you've seen an episode of *COPS*, you know how it's going to end. But *COPS* has been on TV forever, so I guess people don't get sick of it.

Once my character becomes popular, I'll get a movie deal. The movie won't be as good as the comic, but here's my vision for the trailer—that's the movie trailer, which also features the exploding trailer. Check this out.

The screen is dark.

Baritone Voiceover Guy (BVG): As long as the good live in fear . . .

A lightning flash. For an instant we see an aerial shot of Amarillo bathed in white light. The rain pours down. The screen is dark again.

BVG: As long as the unjust prey upon the weak . . .

Another lightning flash. This time it illuminates the wind-swept Llano Estacado. More rain. We see some cattle and a doublewide.

BVG: Only one man can stop them. But until he arrives, you're stuck with . . . the Amarillo Avenger.

Orchestra hit. We see our hero riding a scooter with a bass on his back.

BVG: The Amarillo Avenger, with the power to manipulate frequencies below four hundred hertz.

Then the orchestra hits the throttle, and we see a fast montage: coffee, rain, a scooter chase, a fistfight, changing bass strings, and a love interest of some sort. In the last clip a doublewide explodes.

Marvel or DC, if you're reading this, feel free to contact my people.

LEAVING

W HEN LIFE is going well, I tend to wait for some calamity. I've been doing this since I was nineteen, so by now it's patho-logical.

Before my pop got sick, life was great for our family. He had a job he loved; we were in a nice apartment for once; and Hagfish, the band my brother and I had formed, was doing well. I was nine-teen, in college, and beginning to think I could actually stay and get a degree. I'd become a musicologist and have a good life.

Then my dad went to the hospital with stomach pain. Every-thing changed.

The doctor said my old man had an ulcer. He didn't do any tests. He just wrote him a prescription and sent him away. I had a feeling something worse was going on. The extent of my medical training was that I'd listened to *Dr. Feelgood*, but I just had a feeling.

It turns out antacid is no match for colon cancer. If my dad had gotten the correct diagnosis, they probably could have saved his life. It would have meant more time with his family. He would have met his daughters-in-law. He could have seen me follow through on taekwondo after all these years. But by the time the doctors got it right, the cancer had spread.

He went on chemo and was hopeful, but it just made him sicker and weaker. He was wasting away. After months of that torture, he got word that the cancer was terminal. He said, "I don't want to spend what time I have left being sick." He canceled his hospital appointments and didn't go back until he was on his deathbed.

Before he passed, we gathered in his hospital room. We knew the moment was coming, but that didn't make it any easier. My dad realized he wouldn't live long enough to see his boys grow up, and I think that was the worst part of it for him. It was the only time I saw him cry. My mom and brother left the room, and I stayed behind. He asked—no, demanded—that I be strong for them and always look out for their well-being. I promised I would.

We found ways to move on. You never really get over it, but we had bills to pay, so we had to grieve on our own time.

One lasting repercussion from all that is when life is going well, I get suspicious. I feel like the deer that approaches a feeder in the woods just before he gets shot.

I feel that way now. Life is great, and that worries me.

After twenty-two years of marriage, my wife and I have never been stronger. Work is fine. We love our house. For decades I dreamed of becoming a martial artist. Now I'm training and studying day and night—and I'm writing about it. This is not an extravagant life. It's a good, simple, focused life, and I'm happy.

But there may be a storm out there in the distance.

The Toadies will be heading out on tour soon. It's tough to explain my feelings about this. I love the band, I love the music, and I've always enjoyed the road. But for the first time in my life, I don't want to go on tour. I just don't care.

I worked all my life to play music and tour. Now I'm not excited about it. It's blasphemy, but I only know how I feel, and right now I feel like I should—*gulp*—stay . . . in . . . Amarillo. That seemed impossible just a few years ago, but it's true.

When I decided to pursue taekwondo, I talked about a need to simplify. I was thinking a lot about my dad and wishing I could return to an easier time. I can't bring him back, and I can't travel time, but I do feel like I've simplified my life a bit. Yeah, I still worry about impending doom, but simplifying is relative, and I feel a greater sense of clarity. It's amazing what a new focus will do for you.

That focus, martial arts, gets me out of bed every morning. It's not music—not anymore. With writing and training I have found new creative outlets. I'm not inventing Blair-jitsu here, but martial arts are a way to be expressive. They show the real you. The masters are to martial arts what Mozart is to music. I guess that makes me the Johnny Ramone of taekwondo: blunt, a little ragged, but also loud and effective. I'm cool with that.

It's better than being the Pee-wee Herman of kung fu. I've met that guy, and he sucks.

I have a lot to be excited about. I will make the most of the upcoming tour. I'll kick and punch and train my ass off on the road. When we get home, I have a great job waiting for me at an amazing coffeehouse. I'll get back into rhythm at the local WTF affiliate.

I always tell Shelley we shouldn't worry; we can't predict the future, so we should just prepare for whatever happens and enjoy life. No sense in looking around every corner for the Boogerman, as my grandmother Naomi called him. I will try to take my own advice.

It's always been difficult to leave Shelley. Leaving Amarillo, on the other hand, has been no problem. I've always enjoyed time away from here, but this time will be different. I've never cared for the politics or religion of the Panhandle, but I'm just not fixating on that anymore.

Amarillo, as I have said, is home. I think of it every morning when I get up. Sunrise in the Panhandle is breathtaking and the closest thing to a religious experience I will admit to. Hues of orange and yellow, violent tints of purple-red explode from the east and up into the clouds. It's as if all of the missiles at Pantex went off at once, and you're awarded one last beautiful vision before death.

THE DROP-IN, PART 1: DENTON

I LOVE traveling because it's the best way to learn. There's only so much you can discover when you're stuck at home. Anytime you think you know something, you should take it out into the world and test it. Travel brings endless opportunities for breakthroughs and progress.

I mean, just imagine if Columbus had stayed in Spain with no ambition beyond hanging out and drinking port. We wouldn't have that crappy holiday no one cares about, and nobody would have discovered that continent where all those people already lived.

Bad example. Let's start again.

The Toadies began a tour in Denton, Texas, home of the University of North Texas, the best jazz college west of Boston. There are, ironically, no jazz clubs in town, but there are plenty of cowboy bars, and we were booked to play one. Anytime we have a gig in that sort of place, I'm afraid we'll find ourselves in Bob's Country Bunker from *The Blues Brothers*.

Elwood: Uh, what kind of music do you usually have here?
Bartender: Oh, we got both kinds. We got country *and* Western.

We had played that venue before, and I couldn't help but notice the taekwondo school next door. I always wanted to stop in, say hello, maybe work out with them. I dream of a world like that, one where you can just walk into a dojang anywhere, and people will welcome you. It's a martial exchange. You train together, share ideas, and offer some insight. When it's over, you shake hands, and everyone walks away richer for the experience.

After all, you're on the path of the martial artist, so you recognize that in others. Although you train in different towns and maybe even speak different languages, you know you're in this together, so the little stuff that separates you is just that: little stuff. Taekwondo unites you and your fellow travelers.

I also dream of peace in the Middle East, so . . . you know.

The school was cozy. I was amazed that they could do anything in such a tiny space. I'm used to the local WTF affiliate, and even my grandmaster's small room is bigger than that one.

The group was, well, intimate. There were only a handful of students, and two sisters were taking their first class. The instructor, an American guy of about fifty, had white hair and kind of a potbelly. He led them through what was supposed to be Basic 1. Whatever taekwondo federation you belong to, Basic 1 is your first form. As he instructed the new students, I watched his higher belts practice kicks.

Eh, not so much. This is taekwondo; we're talking about the leading weapons of the art. I watched two black belts throw uninspired kicks. I knew green belts in Amarillo who had more skill.

I don't mean to be so negative. It's just my honest assessment. I study martial arts in person, on video, and in books. I see people who are nothing short of amazing, and I give them full marks.

The other side of it is that I see a lot of people who are lacking, myself included. Once you enter the world of martial arts, you can't help but assess the skills of others—and your own. The good news is that you can learn something from everyone.

It's the same as being in a band. You hear great musicians, and you hear crappy musicians. Just a fact. I cannot listen to a band in a live setting anymore without judging each player and the group as a whole—immediately.

A few years back I attended a church service with my wife. It means something to her. I was trying to be a good husband. They had a "praise band," a bunch of dudes who played Christian rock, and there was no way in hell I could ignore their lack of rhythm, melody, and time. As a whole, they sucked. As individuals, they sucked—and they didn't listen to their bandmates, who sucked.

My wife was involved in the pastor's message. I wasn't. It was impossible for me. Every ten seconds I'd interrupt with "Oh my God. That drummer needs to find the one," or "That guitar is out of tune, and the guy doesn't even know it." That, to me, is a crime far more horrible than the ones Satan perpetrated against humanity.

We never went back. Now my wife attends church online.

Back to Denton. I mentioned that the instructor was an American, and I feel like most Americans don't have much patience. Don't bitch at me for cultural generalizations. Some generalizations are true. The students are in a hurry, and the instructors are too, so get them on the martial arts conveyor belt, take their money, and keep them moving.

The teacher's style was direct but easygoing, which is pretty much the opposite of the grandmaster's. That's not to say the grandmaster is a slave driver—well, I guess he is at times—but I have found that Koreans don't do a lot of explaining. That is another cultural generalization. Start a petition if you don't like it.

This is the Korean way: they show you how to do it, and you get it right by doing it thousands of times.

I hear a lot of talk about "real" martial arts and "traditional" styles. People make a lot of claims. If there's one thing I know for sure about martial training, it's that you must have patience. This is not negotiable. If you want to do this right, it takes a long, long time. We'd all love to have natural physical talent, but you can even approximate that . . . through patience.

The instructor in Denton seemed determined to teach fast and take off. I don't think this is any way to treat new students. It was the sisters' first class, and they were not only learning a form but two advanced kicks and punches. Koreans wouldn't drop all of that on you at once. Learn a little, get a taste for it, and if you come back, good. Now learn a little more.

This is also a good way to vet the students. What if a new student leaves his first class, walks up the street thinking he's Jackie Chan, and knocks someone out just because he can? It's dangerous, and as the teacher, that person's actions will reflect on you.

The instructor realized he had a stranger in the waiting room, and he looked my way a few times. When class was finished, he walked over, extended his hand, and asked my name. That was a good start. I said I was playing music next door, and I just wanted to watch a class. I mentioned that I'm a taekwondo student in Amarillo.

After that, he started giving one-word answers, and it was pretty clear I was not welcome there. Did he know the grandmaster? Did he dislike him? Was he jealous? I couldn't say for sure.

I can say, however, that I'm tired of meeting other martial artists and getting nothing but attitude. It happens all the time. We're in this adventure together, and we're all going through the same things. Why the divisiveness?

I say this as a man who just disclosed his propensity for judging musicians—and martial artists. But I don't think I'm being a hypocrite, and here's why: if the praise band had come down off the stage to talk with me, I would have been decent to them. I didn't admire their skills, but I'll bet we could have had a conversation and gotten along. Same deal with pretty much anyone at the school in Denton. The instructor wasn't interested in that. It's his school, and he can do what he wants, but I don't think that's the way to treat others.

I didn't want to say something I'd regret, and I sure didn't want it to get ugly, so I decided to leave. I had a packed country and Western venue filled with rock 'n' rollers to appease.

And no, I didn't see the taekwondo teacher at the show. I didn't think that was why he was in a hurry.

I'm not an instructor, but I think someday I would like to teach. That's why I take these incidents to heart. There has to be a better way to treat one another. I hold out hope for a world where we welcome other martial artists, regardless of where they're from, where they're headed, and where they are on the path.

And if that's a lost cause, I guess there's always peace in the Middle East.

A MAN'S GOT TO KNOW
HIS LIMITATIONS

YOU CONFRONT your own limitations every time you train. This never stops, and it's something I love about martial arts. The first barrier I had to overcome was that initial call to the grandmaster. Then came the challenge of walking in for class. But even after you get into the rhythm of training, you keep taking on new challenges. You deal with little problems—"Was my thumb in the right place on that punch?"—and sometimes you take on bigger problems: "Do I suck at taekwondo? Should I just give up?"

You see your classmates' progress, and even if you're not especially competitive, you strive to keep up. Away from the dojang, you practice on your own, always pushing ahead. When you find a limitation, you make a note. If it's about flexibility, you work on it, and it improves. If it has to do with an old war injury, it might not get better, so you learn to accommodate. When it's a matter of psychology or disposition, you can only deny that for so long. Eventually, training clarifies who you are, and who doesn't want that?

Well, it does carry certain dangers. You won't always like what you see.

The other night I was sparring with Sam. He landed a round-house kick to my chin. We're not talking a knockout blow, but it was good contact, and getting struck in the face made my vision go red. I clocked him in the head and then dealt a few kicks to his midsection. He returned in kind, and we were off. The grand-master pulled us apart.

These things don't happen much in the office, where the greatest conflict may involve copy-machine etiquette. They do happen in the dojang. You make amends, learn, and move on. Within five minutes Sam and I were friends again. He forgave me sixty times because that was how many times I apologized. I still couldn't sleep that night. You make a note of something like that as well.

I have written about "class fright" and my reluctance to work out in front of normal people. By *normal* I mean people who don't pay monthly dues to get kicked in the face. Even after all this training, I remain a taekwondo introvert. It is another limitation, so I forced myself to confront it.

The other night we were in Phoenix. I'd been cramped in the bus for fifteen hours, and I needed to put some life in my limbs, so I decided to face my old fear. I went to a fantastic gym with a spacious aerobics room. The place was dim, which was perfect for me. One other person was working out there; normally, that would be enough to make me bail, but I forced myself to stay. I stretched out, loosened up, and began working through my forms.

I went through Basic 1 through 3, then Taegeuk 1 through 8. I did them slowly, almost at tai chi tempo.

Guess what happened. Nothing. At all.

The other guy in the aerobics room didn't judge me. He didn't stop to take video to show everyone and tell what a spaz I am. He didn't care. He did his thing, and I did mine. I was so engaged in my workout that I barely noticed when a few more people walked in.

I went through my forms again, picking up the pace. No meltdown. No heart attack. I felt just fine, so I started shadowboxing, upping the intensity with jabs, kicks, and combos. Nobody cared. We were all there for our own reasons, and we were not worried about what anyone else was doing.

My fear of training in front of others might sound silly, but it was real nonetheless. I faced it and overcame it. The workout was great, but the newfound freedom was way better.

Near the end of my session, I started practicing tornado kicks, and that's when everyone took off. It might have been a coincidence, or it might be that when the bearded hobo-looking guy starts throwing flying kicks, that's the cue to split. Either way, I don't care. I overcame another limitation.

Now if I could just pee with someone at the urinal next to me without saying to myself, "Use the force, Luke." Then I'd be normal.

REALITY CHECK

ONCE worked in Dallas at a place called Tapemasters. This was not my big break in the music industry. I packaged cassettes and CDs all day, every day. It was menial and dumb. The band names and the artwork changed—a little—but everything else was the same. You wouldn't believe all the moronic album covers I saw in my tenure as a Tapemaster. It was staggering. We tell kids not to judge a book by its cover, but with just a glance, you could see the creativity and intellect that went into most of those records. Usually, there wasn't much of either.

The album covers were painfully stupid and came in an endless succession. The typical one showed a gaggle of graying middle-aged men gathered on a hilltop. They looked winded from the climb. They wore an assortment of faded Harley Davidson and Metallica T-shirts, and their records usually had titles like *Gettin' Ready*, *Hittin' the Streets*, and *Wheels Up*. The back covers normally featured a girl in a sultry pose, wearing one of the band's T-shirts.

She would almost certainly be some band member's old lady—and that description is as apt as they come.

Others CDs were just enraging. A lot of cover bands played in Dallas, and for promotional purposes, they made records of their repertoire. They wanted to show they could be effective party bands. Their requisite photo always seemed to have five to seven people, men and women, dressed in tuxes and evening gowns. They taped up balloons and party favors, doing their damnedest to bring an air of frivolity to the photo shoot. You'd see some bald dipshit in Ray-Bans playing air saxophone while the others crossed their eyes and made goofy faces. Yet another mental defective would be in the corner wearing a shirt and no pants, shrugging with his hands in the air as if to say, "How did this wacky thing happen?"

The worst ones were the people who did solo albums. The photo was usually black and white, and all the text was cursive, of course, to demonstrate that asshole's class and sophistication. Then you'd see said asshole leaning sideways on the piano. One memorable record was *Self-Titled*. Some jackoff actually called his record *Self-Titled*. This was another standard move: if the guy's name were, say, Aaron Caulfield, then the record would be *Simply Aaron*.

God. Is there any other?

Sometimes we would hurl these albums against the wall like Frisbees.

My coworkers and I got five dollars an hour. We all hated the job. One form of revenge was what we called the five-dollar shit.

Just think about it.

Tapemasters didn't feel like the music business I'd dreamed of, but it did pack some important lessons. Namely, there's no 401K in music. There's no insurance and definitely, as Mr. Rotten put it, no future—that is, unless you're Taylor Swift's vocal coach or you write cheesy pop songs for boy bands. That should mean job security.

If you work hard and have some luck, you make records that end up in classier facilities than Tapemasters. If you find yourself among the chosen few, you get to hit the road in a bus, play every-where, meet weird and interesting folks, and make more than five dollars an hour. It's an education. I was a moron until I toured the world; now I'm a well-traveled moron.

Donivan Blair: Tapemasters alumnus. (Photo by Karlo X. Ramos)

But the touring lifestyle doesn't validate me as a musician or define me as a person. It never has, and I refuse to allow it that power over me. I always want to play my best, but playing is a short part of the day. Touring bands have so much downtime that it's no wonder they can't stay out of trouble.

I am training my ass off on this tour. The other night we got rained out in Clarksburg, West Virginia. The band and crew took off to visit a friend's bar. I don't drink—I work out—so I was alone on the bus. I didn't feel like training in the pouring rain, although that would have made a good scene for a martial arts movie. I sized up the open spaces in the bus and thought I would try working out there.

The bunk area is not what you'd call roomy. The aisle isn't much bigger than shoulder width. This is just where you store the humans to recharge them. I practiced my roundhouse kicks there. Leg

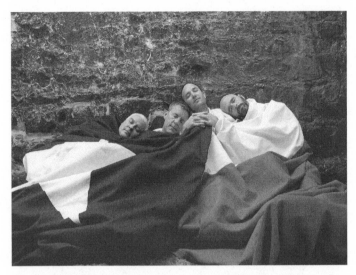

The Toadies: Mark "Rez" Reznicek, Vaden Todd Lewis, Clark Vogeler, and ODB. When we pass through customs at the US border and they ask my citizenship, I say Texan. (Photo by Dylan Hollingsworth)

up, tight against the body, snap it out, and snap it back. Don't kick the hardwood sides or bottoms of the bunks.

This, for me, is the reality of touring. It's not what you see in videos or movies. Sex, drugs, and rock and roll? I guess for some. When I'm traveling, it's taekwondo, books, and rock and roll. I know that sucks the allure and the danger right out of it, but it's the truth.

Another reality of touring comes when it dawns on you that, for the next several months, you'll spend most of your time in a confined space with a bunch of dudes. Won't that be nice? For the Toadies and company, the party hits a crescendo around three A.M. The guys ring in "loud thirty," which is tons of fun—unless you're the dorky straight-edge bassist preoccupied with getting enough rest to be sharp for a morning workout.

For a while I tried taking a melatonin supplement. It helped me sleep through the tornado that is a Toadies party, but it can also kill your libido, which is a problem when you come home after a few months away. You want to show your wife how much you missed her; instead you drop your drawers and hear the "you lose" horns from *The Price Is Right*.

Lesson learned. Dump the melatonin, and tell the guys to kindly shut the fuck up.

Our hotel rooms have been decent on this trip: good beds and furniture but way too many ottomans and chairs for a makeshift dojang. I push everything aside to practice kicks and forms. I train before sound check and get in a second session afterward.

I figure earning a black belt means practicing everywhere and at every opportunity. It takes ingenuity, creativity, and other words that end in *-ity*. I have to be worthy when test time comes. I don't want to be *adequate*. Who respects adequacy? Have you ever described your heroes as *sufficient*?

I'm sure not going to buy my way to black. That does happen. *CoughcoughElvis*.

Here's another disturbing tendency among martial artists: once they become black belts, they quit. They think they've reached the ultimate, so they give up. "Done. Next."

But having a black belt doesn't mean your work is done. It means you've reached a level where the real learning begins. You've proven your dedication and earned the faith of your master. Why quit then? You have to prove it to someone else?

Once you reach black, there are a few more forms to learn—way more advanced forms. Otherwise, there's really not anything new; it's all about refining your technique. That's what I enjoy about taekwondo. Most styles will throw on an added level of kicks and blocks. Not ours. It's all about honing your skill and perfecting your form.

This is a big responsibility. Every move has to reflect the level of the belt you have around your waist. No more sloppy strikes. No more "Oh, I forgot how to do that." No excuses, damn it. If you think you have any reason to hold back, please drop your belt where you stand, and get the fuck out.

I've decided that I want to continue on this journey and maybe one day reach the rank of master. If I keep training hard, I might be able to pull that off by the time I hit fifty-two. That sounds like another book in the making.

LET ME OFF THIS DAMN BUS

You've seen images of meteors entering our atmosphere, hunks of rock blazing orange and blue and green, hurtling toward the Earth at a hundred thousand miles an hour. Heat increases. Fragments fall away. A furious stone crashes into the planet and scars the land. What remains is just a smoldering core of what was.

This is how I feel.

You might think I'm about to make an analogy for training. I'm not. It's true that overdoing your training, something I know too much about, can leave you utterly depleted. But what has me worried is that I'm burned out on being a touring musician.

I should not make this confession. Getting anywhere in music is an impossible long shot. You need some mystical combination of talent, determination, timing, fashion, and luck—and not necessarily in that order. If you do become a career musician, if you're one of the chosen few, you have to express your undying gratitude to anyone and everyone who helps make it possible.

Well, I am grateful.

But I'm also missing from my marriage, and I have been for way too long. Touring leaves you lonely and disconnected from the ones you love, and even though Shelley and I talk every day, I'm still absent in mind and heart. Listen to "Talking" by the Descendents; that's pretty much a heart punch: "I'm out here alone / Talking on the phone / Maybe we'll fall in love when I get home."

In my career I've been away for too many gigs and too many tours. My wife feels like she comes in second. Nothing could be further from the truth, but she feels that way, and I can see why. When your husband has missed your first, fifth, tenth, and fifteenth anniversaries because he had to "take the music to the people," you might begin to feel slighted.

Shelley and I watch from the side of the stage. This is the night before I hit the road for three months. (Photo by Lauren Basset)

I need to be present and focused to deliver for the band. I need to be present and focused to be a good husband. Sometimes I fail at both. For the past twenty-something years I have tried and failed to be in two places at once. I've been the rope in this tug-of-war.

I'm writing this on the bus. We've had several sellouts lately, and I should be thrilled. In truth, I couldn't be bothered to care. I used to live for the road and making music, but I'm not having any fun on this tour, at least not right now. This is a fact I can't ignore.

Shelley has been distant of late, and a short call or FaceTime chat is just not enough to fix the problem. What could improve the situation? Well, having her fucking husband home for longer than two weeks at a time might help. I feel like she's shutting down toward me. We've talked about it before, and it's how she copes with my being gone so much. It's easier that way. Whatever helps her, OK I get it. I have no choice.

I haven't been able to focus on anything. Am I succumbing to pressure from home? Possibly. Is this affecting my performance and enthusiasm? Of course. But it's not her fault. She can't help but vent to me. I'm her only outlet, but I have none of my own. My only avenue to express this is this stupid journal that's written so badly I'm sure it will never see the light of day.

My enthusiasm for the road has waned because I've realized I need to fucking grow up. There's making music, which I will always do, and then there's being a big boy and doing what needs to be done. I've battled this my entire career: am I being a good husband by being home and earning nothing, or am I being a good husband by doing whatever I can to earn a living? It has perplexed me for years.

Now I'm tired. I'm burned out.

This year has been a long, hard one for our family. The wear and tear from my "job" does not help. I feel alone despite the fact that I'm constantly around people. My wife is the only person I relate to, but even that can change. Will she forgive me for leaving

My shadow: taller than my soul.

her alone for months on end? Will she ignore me until I get home and deal with it then?

I could talk to my brother, but Zach isn't what you would call open-minded about leaving the business and getting a straight. Whenever I've tried to bring it up, he's just lectured me about quitting. He has such fervor for the ideal. But he's also a lot more talented than I am. Acknowledging that isn't giving up; it's just being honest. He won't hear it. So, no, I can't talk about this with him.

New bands go on the road and starve. They return home broke or in debt, but they accept that just to get in front of crowds. They have to deliver every night because every performance is another investment in their business. I know saying it that way takes the myth and magic out of rock and roll, but that's just the reality. With more recording and more touring, they might begin to finish in the black. Maybe.

Shelley and I got married in our early twenties. I'd go on tour and get home with a couple of bucks in my pocket. I felt miserable. I'd start looking for a day job, all the while trying to make up for lost time with her. Not once did she complain. I always had her support, and I still do, but now there is a weariness attached.

The Toadies are not a new band, and we're not willing to do that starter shit. But no matter what you're making, when you add in the time, the hours confined on a bus, and the personal costs, it becomes far less. If I made Metallica money, Shelley and I would never worry about finances again, and maybe that would justify the time away. But maybe even then it wouldn't.

So why do this? Should I put my marriage and my wife under all this strain just to play rock and roll? Lately I'm not a good band member to be around either, so that adds to the pressure.

If this had boiled over a few years ago, I would have gone into epileptic fits trying to find some way to keep playing music. But now I need to defend my marriage, and since I've found a new purpose in taekwondo, I'm reconsidering everything. Martial arts have made me a better husband and a better man. My main ambition now is to go home, train, and get coffee with my wife on a Saturday morning. That's more fulfilling than touring.

I make a distinction between touring and playing. I can and will play music for the rest of my life. That's a given. Will I be touring for the rest of it? That's the question. Right now I don't know. The way I feel might be nothing more than a visit from my emo alter ego. But it could be the moment I decide to make a change.

I have a little side project back home, a surf band called the Mag Seven. Why not start a surf band in the middle of Texas? In 1998 I became obsessed with the idea. I called up some friends, and we've been together ever since. In nearly twenty years we have sold fewer records than Chris Gaines, but we have reached audiences. People have heard us in the background of *Road Rules* and *MTV*

Cribs, among other shows. We continue recording, people continue not caring, and we continue having fun anyway.

Maybe I'll leave the Toadies. Maybe I'll get a day job and be a Texas surf rocker on weekends. We could just book gigs in the cities nearby. We'd have fun, play some good songs, and get back home to our families. On Monday morning I'd punch the clock again.

I realize the irony here. The guys who are home playing bars wish they were on a tour bus. I'm on a tour bus, wishing I were home playing bars. I'd like to be in one place and have a decent day job. I want to leave the office for the afternoon, go to the dojang, and make it home in time for dinner—and yes, a romp with the wife.

Anytime I told other musicians that I want out of the touring life, they looked at me like I threw up in their mouths.

We are on I-10 now, headed to LA—Shaky Town. This is what I dreamed of as a kid. But right now I'm dreaming of a life with no meet-and-greets. No radio visits. No eight-hour bus rides or detours or gigs in the middle of nowhere.

The first person I see in the morning is usually Wes, our tour manager and guitar tech. That's just not right. I love Wes, but life has got to get better than this.

THE DROP-IN,
PART 2: LOS ANGELES

ONE PERK of traveling is that you have the chance to check out shops, libraries, and museums everywhere you go. I know all the bookstores, record stores, and comic shops back home. I go in, buy what I went for, and leave. When I'm on tour, though, it's Christmas. I go places I've never been and see things I may never see again. It's like a line from a Willie Nelson song. Why not drop in? Who knows what you'll find inside? Every store welcomes street traffic, so why wouldn't a martial arts school be the same?

If you're a martial artist, you may already be laughing about this notion. It turns out a lot of these places run like secret societies. Walk in the front door—if it's unlocked—and it's like the KGB has opened a file on you.

But it gets rather boring jumping over chairs in your hotel room, punching the mitts your drummer is nice enough to hold, and kicking your singer in the head while he sleeps. I would never visit another school back in Amarillo, but, you know, what happens in Vegas stays in Vegas. Or in this case Los Angeles.

The Toadies had a day off, and I hate days off. I want to work and train and write, and I detest wasting time. I only feel like I've earned some rest when we've finished a run of six straight days of shows. And even then I will probably work out.

We had been booked every day, so a little downtime felt good. I planned to do laundry, get in a workout, treat myself to a nice dinner at Olive Garden—I'm a big spender who knows how to live—and then catch a movie. That's a good day for me. I'm a simple guy, a cheap date, and a frugal man.

I did a little research and discovered there was a taekwondo school just a block from my hotel. Rejoice!

I walked down to the school and asked the woman at the front desk if they accepted walk-ins. She introduced me to the head instructor. My first impression? Bulky. He looked like so many of the martial arts instructors I've seen over the years: big, pumped-up dudes. I have yet to figure out this fascination. It must be short-man syndrome because, as far as I can tell, it makes no sense from a martial perspective. These people make their living from a discipline that requires speed, agility, and flexibility, and yet they want to look like bodybuilders. Ever heard of Bruce Lee? Anybody?

The sign said taekwondo, but the instructor recited the usual amalgam-of-styles bullshit. Hardly anyone "just" practices one art. You have to study taekwondo for the kicks, judo for the throws, Brazilian jiu-jitsu for the chokes, boxing for the footwork, Jeet Kune Do for the one-inch punch, krav maga for the headbutts, and *lucha libre* for the diving double axe handle. It's so complicated.

The guy had a mustache, which was another strike against him. Maybe not the mustache per se, but the way he tapped it with one finger while considering my request—and he considered it awhile, which annoyed me. Say yes or no, but don't flex your authority.

To fill the silence, I told him about my training. I was no newbie. I was a red belt, which I thought was pretty damn impressive.

"Hmm." Tapping mustache.

Finally he relented, and I was in for the night. "Enough with the passive aggression," he must have thought. "Let's get on with the aggressive aggression."

Here's the lesson I was about to learn: never brag about your rank. Why would I do that? I don't know when to shut the hell up.

This guy ran us into the floor for the next two hours. My class back home is tough. It's a hell of a workout. But that night, Sifu Mustache brought the pain. Even his higher ranks were sweating and panting. I'm positive he thought, "OK, hotshot, let's see what you got," and the whole class paid for my presence.

First he took us through conditioning and plyometric drills that would have made the Flash surrender. Then we moved to sparring. It hurt and I said ow a lot. I faced off with a higher belt and got my ass kicked so bad that they called for a green belt. Still got my ass kicked. I forgot how mean thirteen-year-old girls can be.

I liked to believe I was in pretty good shape for a guy my age, or any age for that matter. I could handle a lot of punishment. But good God, I've never been in as much pain as when I hobbled out of that place. These people probably trace their style of taekwondo back to Sparta.

After class the instructor was smiling, unlike his students, and he thanked me for coming.

"Did you have any difficulties with anything?" he said.

"No," I said. "I feel great. Lots of fun and I learned a lot."

His smile disappeared. "Good. Please come back anytime."

"Oh definitely," I said. I forced one last smile. Even that hurt.

My face was a rictus of forced pleasure until I hit the door. I limped back to the hotel. It took 120 counts of "Why?" and 235 of "Goddamnitthathurtsomuch" to get there. Then I applied heaping quantities of Bengay—can you put Bengay on your face?—and I made a whimpering call to my wife.

That was my day off. No pasta. No movie. No mercy.

BLAIR VS. THE FRIGIDAIRE

W<small>E WERE</small> arguing. That's how this all began.

When Shelley and I aren't getting along, we usually just go to separate corners. No reason to yell about shit that honestly doesn't matter. It's wasted time, and it can put dents in your marriage. We just ignore each other for an hour or so, and when we reconvene, everything's OK.

Not so this time. It was not good.

This particular disagreement sent me spiraling through the past. It was scary.

If you have parents, you've heard them argue. You've heard them say awful things to each other—or, I should say, *at* each other. It's not a conversation; it's a sparring match. And maybe that's not just a metaphor. Maybe you've seen them launch plates and clocks and phones at each other. Maybe you've seen one hit the other.

You never forget that stuff. Even decades later, it returns in your nightmares, and you're seven years old, curled up beneath your blanket, helpless all over again.

I remember the times my brother and I were in our beds at night and the yelling would begin. We lived in shit apartments with Sheetrock walls. We could hear everything. I'm sure the neighbors could too.

From left to right: me, my mom, Zach, and an electrical outlet.

Often the commotion would stop there—just angry words and a slamming door. Other times it would escalate. I'd hear strikes, impacts of some sort. I can't say for certain who or what was getting hit. Maybe the walls. Maybe my mom. Maybe my dad. Mom was no wallflower. She wouldn't have cared about having a two-hundred-fifty-pound monster for an opponent. Taking shit from anyone was not her style. Whatever was going on, I was too scared to leave the room. I never saw my parents hit each other; I just might have heard it.

They argued about money. Every time. My folks were under constant pressure to make rent, feed us, and put gas in our myriad of cars that never worked. My mom and dad were products of the sixties and the days of free love. Love, love, love. Love was all you needed. No need to get a job like your square parents. No reason to have a bank account and save money. I've heard that love is patient and kind and blind and that it conquers all. Well, it sure as hell doesn't pay the rent.

When my parents' jobs couldn't cover our monthly expenses, we had to explore other options. We borrowed from my grandparents. We scrutinized our belongings to see what we could pawn next. Can we live without the TV until the next paycheck? Can we live without it for good? I was twelve, and I had no idea why everyone was freaking out about the Super Bowl. Oh well. I'd watch it next season.

Without my grandparents' financial help and our circuit of pawnshops, we would have lived on welfare like a lot of our neighbors.

We did lean on the state for food. Sometimes we went to food banks and stood in line for God-awful government cheese. We signed up for SNAP, Supplemental Nutrition Assistance Program. Texas food stamps were supersized in the eighties. The idea was to shame you for using them, and it worked. When you pull out food stamps the size of greeting cards, you feel like scum for trying to

Donald and Patricia Blair.

feed your family. But we had to eat, and humility was a luxury we could not afford.

We lived in a succession of beater apartments. You've seen the kind: surrounded by a gate in disrepair, No TRESPASSING signs, No LOITERING signs, UNDER NEW MANAGEMENT signs. People in that social stratum require a lot of signs.

Day and night you see dirty kids running around, playing with worn-out toys and riding broken-down bikes. I was one of those dirty kids. My bike was so bad that I once went over a speed bump, fell, and racked my nuts on the bar. Then the bar split in two.

Did my brother laugh? His ass off.

Did my dad buy me a new bike? Welding was cheaper.

Despite all our scrimping and scrounging, there were still funds for the monthly beer budget. Beer is the lifeblood of working-class Texas. You can't fix a car without it, you can't go hunting without it, and you sure as shit can't watch the Cowboys without it. Olympus has nectar and Texas has beer.

My parents were quite fond of the stuff, the way it alleviated their stress and lubricated their tongues. Weekends in particular meant alcohol. It eased the pressure, but only until the fighting started. And it always started.

My mom has a fiery temper and a loud mouth. She is Irish and Cherokee Indian. Throw firewater into the mix, and you can probably guess the results. My dad's anger was a slow burn, a searing ember you dare not touch. My mom's was that one Mexican firework with a really short fuse. *¡Chingado!*

Sorry to say it, but I take after her. I've tried and tried to develop more restraint, but the truth is, in the wrong situation, I can still go from zero to Patricia Blair in three seconds flat.

I say all of this to provide a little context. It's not an excuse. My parents weren't perfect, but they taught me to be accountable for my actions. When I screw up, I own it. Hell, I'll even confess it in a book. Here goes.

We were arguing. That's how this all began.

I'd been on tour for months, and Shelley was home with our dog, Frank. She works at home, so aside from phone calls with me, he was her only companion. One evening, after working all day, walking Frank three times, and feeding and cleaning up after him, she went online and saw pictures of her husband between two girls. Or maybe she saw photos of the boobs I had signed. It's a job hazard.

When I finally got home, I was expecting a hero's welcome. Kisses. Adoration. The shedding of clothes. Instead I got a screaming fury. All work and no play while your husband's off living the life. I get it, but it caught me off guard at the moment.

OK, the truth is I lost my shit. I just wanted to hold her, and instead I punched the goddamn fridge.

If there's any good news here, it's that it was an excellent punch. After all this time in training, I've developed my punch so the points of impact are just the first two knuckles. You get a more focused strike that way, and you're less likely to injure your hand. That's important if you, oh, I don't know, play a musical instrument for a living.

Seriously, what would I have told the band if I'd broken my hand beating up an appliance?

I'm disgusted with myself over this. I'm also disgusted that I think it's cool that I dented a freaking fridge and it didn't hurt my hand.

I'd never hit my wife. I'd never hit any woman. But I do have a history of tossing housewares and boxing with inanimate objects. I'm not proud of this. I'd hoped it would stay in the distant past. Training in martial arts has taught me a great deal about managing my anger. I thought I was getting somewhere. But no, I have a long way to go.

Martial artists like to talk about balance, about staying cool in volatile situations. We quote Bruce Lee: "Be formless, shapeless, like water." We quote the *Dao Teh Ching*: "A good soldier is never aggressive; A good fighter is never angry."[2]

That's all deep and meaningful and everything—until someone hits a raw nerve and you're just fucking furious. Then what?

If you're a martial artist, if you really embody these values, then nothing. Then you breathe. That's it.

If you're faking it, you punch the fucking fridge.

I am a goddamn red belt now. I'm supposed to be better than this.

---

2. Lao Tzu, *Dao Teh Ching*, trans. John C. H. Wu (Boston: Shambhala, 1990).

INSOMNIAC BOXING

AT NIGHT we get to discover a world we don't see in the daytime. It's not like this alternate reality just springs from the ether because the sun has set. It has more to do with our attention. Traffic dies down, the world becomes quieter, and normal people call it a day. The weird and the interesting tend to stick out more: the crazy lady in a poncho talking to herself, hot rods flying down the strip at breakneck speed, groups of homeless asleep in a field by the railroad tracks. When the Earth turns its back on the sun, another world comes out. This is the one my dad preferred.

Don was an insomniac by nature, which was perfect when he worked as a late-night DJ on the radio. He was a loner, and that influenced all his interests. He liked sports and games you could play by yourself, such as billiards, golf, and solitaire. He said, "In team sports, you have to rely on people. Don't ever put yourself in a situation where you have to count on another person."

Being on the radio late at night gave him the freedom he needed. He played what he wanted when he wanted, ratings be damned.

Callers from all over the Sherman-Denison listening area made the weirdest requests and he loved filling them. "South Side of the Sky" at four in the morning? Why the hell not? Why not play an entire side of Pink Floyd's *Meddle*? Who was going to stop him?

My pops spent his nights off much the same way, staying up, playing records with headphones on, and enjoying the solitude. He wasn't able to turn off his nocturnal nature just because it was a night away from the microphone, so he would read whatever was lying around and watch TV. He looked forward to these uninterrupted evenings to explore what was out there. It was the Wild West of late-night television, and what you got was what was on. It could have been the live comedy show *Fridays*, ABC's answer to *Saturday Night Live*—or it could have been midget wrestling. In 1983 he flipped on *Austin City Limits* and discovered a young blues guitarist named Stevie Ray Vaughn.

These were the days before cable TV, at least in the Blair house. We had three channels, which meant even fewer choices at three in the morning, when you were likely to find paid programming and test patterns.

One morning at breakfast my dad told Zach and me about something awesome he had seen the night before. He'd fallen asleep on the couch, but he woke up in time to catch what looked like a boxing match. This, however, was different. Two guys entered the ring wearing gloves, foot guards, and long pants. After trading punches back and forth, they began to kick each other in the face and head. It blew my old man's mind. He was hooked.

Zach and I copied everything my father did, so we had to get a look at kickboxing. My dad perused the *TV Guide* for more matches and discovered that they had a regular slot Sunday at twelve in the morning. My brother and I begged to stay up with him. My mom could not have cared less. She had grown up being forced to watch boxing because my grandfather Noel loved it. Papaw was a lifelong Ali fan. He worshipped the man. Kickboxing wasn't traditional boxing, meaning Noel would hate it—meaning it was A-OK in my mom's book. Zach and I were nine and ten, but we had permission to stay up and watch. It was like joining a secret society, adults only.

Saturday night had always meant watching the Von Erichs, a family that defined professional wrestling in Texas for generations. When we discovered kickboxing, our new heroes became Bill "Superfoot" Wallace and Jean-Yves "The Iceman" Thériault. Like my old man, we were hooked. For us to change that ritual—to watch something other than muscled-up men slamming one another at the Sportatorium—felt like we were cheating on a Texas tradition.

Fuck it. Traditions are made to be broken.

I remember waking up groggy on Sunday mornings because we had spent the night in front of the TV with my pops. Every Sunday we went to visit my mom's parents, Papaw and Mamaw, for lunch. Zach and I would get to talking about the fights we had seen, and we'd get amped up all over again, trying to recreate what we'd witnessed.

My grandfather was not amused. "What the hell are you trying to kick for?" he said. "Just punch like Ali."

"Kicking is cooler, Papaw," I said.

In my ten-year-old brain, I could reason with a sixty-five-year-old man about this. It didn't help. To him, real men fought with their fists. Using your feet was cheating. It also kept you at a farther distance, making it almost impossible to get knocked out. Where was the contest in that?

"If you're afraid to get hit," he said, "you ain't worth shit."

My grandfather had served in World War II. He'd been a policeman and a firefighter. He watched his uncle shoot his aunt and then blow his own brains out. He'd seen his three-year-old brother drop dead from consuming bad moonshine. Papaw was half Cherokee and half Irish, and he'd been involved in more drunken brawls than Conor McGregor. That old fart had never been far from violence, and he wasn't afraid of anything.

Papaw, Noel Harbor, a fighting man.

One of my earliest memories is of Papaw trying to teach us to box. "Put up your dukes," he said. Zach was one and a half. He put his mug in Zach's face and said, "Goo-goo, gaga." Zach had enough and punched him.

The next day Papaw's coworkers asked him where he got the black eye. "My goddamn grandson punched me," he said.

Once Papaw understood his grandsons' zeal for martial arts and anything to do with kicking—especially the shit out of each other—he dropped his distaste for our new passion and supported us. We were forging our own identities, and sometimes you just have to let your freak flag fly.

That's funny because everything my dad did was a freak flag in my grandfather's eyes. Don's music, hair, clothes, and beliefs were the opposite of everything Papaw held dear. The first time he met my father, he asked my mom, "Why are you hanging around with a damn hippie?" His tone softened over the years, as my dad proved how much he loved her, but the men's mutual distrust never left—a cop on one side, a longhair on the other.

The two differed in their views on boxing and kickboxing, but sport fighting at least gave them something to talk about. Instead of dreading the company of his uptight father-in-law, my dad took comfort in the fact that they had something in common.

Ultimately, whether anyone approved of the Blair men's new interest didn't matter much. Hanging out late with my old man, watching kickboxing, that was something special Zach and I shared with him. If I knew then how little time we'd have together, I would have done my best to stay up later.

OUCH: A BRIEF RÉSUMÉ OF PAIN

YOU NEED guts to begin, but it takes wisdom to stop. I got a lot of one and not enough of the other.

Getting hurt is just a fact of training. Striking, grappling, sumo wrestling . . . whatever your discipline, if you're really in this thing, you'll have to learn to work through the pain. Hell, if you were serious about ping-pong—excuse me, table tennis—you'd have to do the same.

Just to clarify, when I say pain, I'm talking about the chronic problems, the stuff that follows you around and affects your quality of life. A fist to the nose or a foot to the cojones is inconvenient, but you'll get over it. If, however, you fuck up your knee, that's going to take a lot longer.

Here's one simple test to measure the significance of an injury. If your wife says, "Do you want to go see a movie?" and you think, "No, because that would require walking," you're probably dealing with chronic pain.

I present this résumé of pain not to impress you but to depress you. This old body isn't exactly falling apart, but it is taking a beating. Take up a martial art, and this fun can be yours too.

I've mentioned the bag room at the local WTF affiliate. That's where my classmates and I usually get hurt, which is why I call it the Dungeon of Death. I train there all the time, but anytime I'm about to walk in, I hesitate. Do I really want to do this?

I've broken my toes and ripped my toenails breaking boards in there. I've mangled my hands, feet, and knees on the Wavemaster bags. The padding is not the problem. It's the plastic base, which I hit with the occasional wild-ass strike. Ow.

One night before I left for the tour, we were working on kicks. I launched a roundhouse, and it landed with a smack. The grandmaster said, "Great kick, Donivan."

"Great?" I thought. "Wow. Great? Does that mean the grandmaster thinks *I'm* great? That wasn't even my best kick. I'll show him what I can really do."

I threw another, missed the bag entirely, and tore my left meniscus.

Other injuries come in a less dramatic way. The unforgiving rubber mat, for example, is stealing my soul. There's no trauma, no outward sign; it's just slow, brutal attrition. It's wrecking my knees and heels. When I go to bed at night, I still feel like I'm standing on that stupid mat. I can feel it in my hips and up my spine. I'd rather we just work out on bare concrete. It would be more comfy.

When I feel an injury coming on, it's hard to know when to stop. I mean, it's not like I'm a personal trainer or anything. Wait a minute. Yeah, I am. The textbooks say rest is just as important as training, but knowing when to stop and forcing myself to do it are two different matters.

The band recently took part in the Summerland tour, an eight-week run. Before we headed out, I put together an Excel spreadsheet listing every World Taekwondo Federation school in every city we would play. I figured I would stop in at as many as possible. I'd get a workout with a certified instructor, which might mean less chance of developing a bad habit or hurting myself. I'd also see a variety of approaches to training. That would be inspiring.

I printed my spreadsheet and presented my findings to the grandmaster, hoping to impress him with my dedication and tenacity. I asked what he thought of my plan. Was it all right to put into action?

He was silent for a full ten seconds. Then he said, "No. Train form instead."

So I did—but I did a whole lot more. I trained every day of the tour. On upper-body days, I focused on punches and blocks, on lower-body days, kicks and forms. To build leg strength I added a hundred squats and a hundred heel lifts.

I even found time to play a little music. Performing in the summer heat is a workout in its own right, but stomping my left foot for forty minutes every night didn't help. My knee and heel ached. I couldn't help it. If you got to play next to a drummer as good as mine, you would stomp too.

All that training has yielded some positive results though. My technique has gotten better, my kicks are sharper and more focused, and I feel stronger overall. One night the band and I were relaxing in the lounge of the bus after the show. We had Steely Dan cranked on the hi-fi, which is a statement likely to divide my readership. I was wearing shorts. My singer Todd yelled, "Holy shit! Look at ODB's legs! They're huge."

ODB is Ol' Doni Blair.

It made me feel good because I had worked hard, weird that my friends were checking out my legs to "The Caves of Altamira," and good again, knowing if a pine board messed with us on the road, I'd be able to take care of business.

Now I'm home, and I've run myself down. Big time. I have a talent for this. I don't know when to stop, I don't know how to stop, and even when I see the reasons to slow down, I can't bring myself to do it. My CHECK ENGINE light came on long ago, but I kept on driving. This is a personal flaw, and it will probably kill me someday.

That's why I've come up with a revolutionary new way of dealing with my own faults: I blame others. It's fantastic. It means I'm always right, and that makes me feel better about myself. If people find out about this technique, I think it's really going to catch on.

Leg injury? Owen's fault.

Broken toe? That's the mat in the Dungeon of Death.

Missed the Wavemaster? Blame the Wavemaster. Or the grandmaster. He never should have complimented me like that.

Overtraining on tour? The grandmaster again. If he had allowed me to visit forty martial arts schools in forty days, I surely wouldn't have overtrained.

Remember that joke from when you were a kid? "I think something's wrong with my eyes. I've been seeing spots."

"Have you seen a doctor?"

"No, just spots."

I had one of those moments when I got back from the tour. I went to the doctor to have him check out my left knee. I told him about the stomping, the jumping, and the taekwondo. I might have mentioned training every day on tour.

"How can I keep my knee from hurting?" I said.

"Stop kicking things," he said.

Right. Sports medicine is not his specialty.

Self-restraint is not mine.

STUDENTS TAKE THE LEAD

L INEAGE IS a big deal in martial arts. People want to know who you are, where you come from, and who you studied with. Who did your master study with? This is about more than just bragging rights; it's about pedigree and the transmission of knowledge. There are some self-taught martial artists in the world, and most of them look like self-taught martial artists. The majority of us still learn the real stuff the old-fashioned way: we stand in front of the master, get our asses kicked, and serve a martial apprenticeship.

I have to admit this apprenticeship has gotten tougher lately. It's not that I'm less committed or that my conditioning has slipped. It's that my classmates and I are getting less and less time with the grandmaster. It seems he's always gone on business.

I don't mean this as a criticism. I have the utmost respect for the grandmaster, his skills, and all that he's accomplished. The guy is the real deal. He has knowledge and expertise that few people in the world have, which is why he's so busy—and why he's just not around enough. He has to attend to his other school, which is near Dallas, five hours away. He coaches Team USA. He judges competitions for the World Taekwondo Federation. Because of all that, we just aren't seeing much of him.

For many instructors, this is the reality of running a martial arts school. They have to be in a lot of places at once. I understand that, but I do get frustrated, and I'm not the only one. It's the reason Conner left the school. Not long after that, Spencer did the same. That sucks. The place is not the same without them.

If there is a bright side here, it's that the students and junior instructors have learned to push ahead on their own. I learn a lot from my classmates, sometimes more than from the grandmaster. They are closer to my skill level—if not my age. I watch them work through their mistakes, and that helps me correct my own.

Eric is a sophomore in high school, and some nights he leads the class. I'd say I'm old enough to be his father, but if I had a kid at twenty, and my kid had a kid at twenty, then I'd have a grandson Eric's age. There's a fucked-up thought for you.

Some kids start young and straighten out their technique early. Eric is one of those, but he has another advantage: he is so damn cerebral. He analyzes and deconstructs way more than most people his age—or people my age, come to think of it. I was fixated on a couple of things when I was fifteen, and the perfect axe kick was not one of them.

Eric is slow and methodical when he breaks down kicks. He makes sure we feel how the hip drives the leg. He shows us the correct placement of the foot. A roundhouse strikes with the top of the foot; a side kick uses the heel as its striking focus, but the toes point toward the ground. These are the general features, but there's so much nuance in getting them just right. You have to fine-tune your balance and weight distribution, the mix of tension and softness, the slightest shifts of the ankle and foot.

Eric gets all of that, which is why I have no problem taking instruction from a fifteen-year-old. The kid could make a living at this if he chooses to.

The biggest lesson I take from Eric is the importance of patience. It's kind of sad that a fifteen-year-old has to teach me to be patient, but I suppose as long as you learn it someday, it doesn't matter who finally gets through.

I returned to taekwondo because I heard my martial biological clock ticking. When I launched myself into it, I was ready for anything, but I really wanted to keep up the pace. I thought, "Lay it on me, and make it fast." But good technique takes so much longer than that. You have to time yourself with a calendar, not a stopwatch.

Given Eric's tendency for analysis, the kid is dialed in for this.

Sam is another student who leads our classes. It's clear that he sees Eric as his rival. Sam is two years older, and though they are both second-degree black belts, he regards Eric as his junior. When Eric tries to lead, Sam feels Eric is usurping him. I guess we should expect this. If a teenager doesn't feel inadequate, he's not a teenager.

Sam shouts commands and loves being in charge. Where Eric leads in concepts, Sam goes for the jugular with murderous all-out cardio stress tests. He's seventeen. He can do it, so he figures everyone can. It doesn't register when the forty-two-year-old guy has collapsed on the mat, clutching his chest.

Enjoy it now, kid. You're nearing the peak of your physical talents. You've got more energy and more stamina than you ever will. In a few years, you'll find the concepts a lot more appealing and the yelling a lot less tolerable.

For kicking drills, we usually do twenty-five repetitions per leg. Sam makes us go to fifty—because he can. It's OK with me. This is what I signed up for. When the other students complain, Sam takes it personally and pouts. A seventeen-year-old is one part little kid, one part adult. It's a funny mix that can be dangerous at times. He'll learn.

Lee also leads the group. He doesn't like to teach, which is a shame because he's really good. He's a smart kid, and he's incredibly gifted physically with his speed and focus.

I struggled for the longest time to get the double roundhouse kick. Imagine that you're in a fighting stance. Usually, you would throw a roundhouse with your rear leg. For the double, you kick twice with the lead instead. First you strike the stomach to make your opponent drop his hands. Then, without bringing the leg back, you deliver a roundhouse to his face, which is unprotected. Very cool technique.

For weeks the grandmaster had been trying to show me this, and for weeks I could not get the timing right. When Lee showed me, I wasn't nervous, probably because I knew no yelling would ensue if I got it wrong. I was just more comfortable with Lee.

Later that evening Lee and I sparred. I danced around, feinted, and threw a few quick shots at his arms. When the time was right, I went for the double and landed it, meaning I kicked him in the face. Lee practically loses his shit when he gets hit in the face, but that time he just laughed it off. It was a credit to his instruction. You can't get mad if you're a good teacher.

Lois teaches Saturday classes, and I always enjoy her lessons. She uses completely different techniques. She has us go to the wall and brace ourselves for kicking drills. Then we throw our legs up as far as possible. I can feel the ligaments tearing. It's fantastic.

Finally, there's this weird guy, Doni, who teaches a little.

I've been able to show my fellow students a few things. Our warm-ups usually last fifteen minutes, but when I lead, they are thirty.

No one complains. The class grunts, cries, and farts, but no one complains. I am a lower rank, but because of my age, I get a certain level of respect. Plus, they all know what an asshole I can be. If anyone gripes, I'll double the repetitions.

It turns out that there are benefits of the grandmaster's time away. We're all learning, taking on new roles, and moving ahead. This shows the importance of training with people who are on it, people who will push you to get better. We share what we've learned, and camaraderie and competition keep us moving.

I'm happy about that, but lately I am having my doubts. When I came back to taekwondo, I didn't expect that one of my teachers would be fifteen years old. Eric is awesome, and I'm glad to train with him. But if the grandmaster isn't going to be around, I have to wonder about my future in his school.

I HAD A DAD

IN A few months I will turn forty-four—the same age as my father when he died from colon cancer.

I keep wondering how to describe Donald W. Blair. It's complicated. The man was a mass of contradictions. He was quiet, but he had plenty to say. He was opinionated, but he rarely offered unsolicited advice. He wasn't religious, but he read the Bible three times. He wanted my brother and me to stay out of trouble, but he loathed conformity. I was a punk kid with long hair, and when I cut it to get a job at Domino's, the old man was angry with me. I was seventeen and I just wanted to raise enough gas money so my brother and I could go to Dallas on the weekends and play in a band. My dad saw my short hair and said, "You're kowtowing to the man."

When he was a kid, my dad encountered his share of danger and misadventure. Once he got too close to an old-school bathroom heater. In those days heaters had open flames, and people weren't thinking much about flame-retardant clothing. His pajamas caught fire, giving him third-degree burns before my grandmother put him out. He was five years old.

When he was twelve or thirteen, Donald took a turn at bat in a neighborhood baseball game with his pals. His eyesight was never good, and he wore glasses, but his parents couldn't afford sports lenses. The pitcher lost control of a fastball and hit Donald in the right eye. The glass shattered and he never saw with that eye again.

In his life my dad went through the windshields of three different cars.

These sound like tall tales, but they are true.

As a man my dad was 250 pounds and strong, but he was sensitive and kind. He managed a wholesale flower shop and brought my mom roses every week. Late one Christmas Eve, he went by a gas station to fill up his delivery van before heading home to us. The cashier was by herself, and I guess it killed him to see her away from family, working on a holiday. He went out to the van and got her a dozen roses. He said Merry Christmas and left. Later we found out he did this all over town. He never mentioned it to anyone, especially my mom. That would have ruined what he had done.

Then again, I witnessed that same man beat someone almost to death. A drunk guy—we'll call him Glen—was at our apartment one night. He pulled my mother's hair when my dad had stepped out. Once he got word, my dad found Glen, launched him over his head into a ditch, and drove him into the ground with a flying suplex. Then he punched him so many times that he smashed Glen's orbital bones. The guy almost lost his left eye.

Alcohol figured into most of my dad's problems. He drank a lot. For much of my childhood he was unable to keep a job. We went to the pawnshop on a regular basis, just so we could afford to eat. We found a way. We were together, we had meals together, and we had a roof over our heads. That's family.

Yeah, I had to hock my stereo once or twice, and I wouldn't have chosen that, but, you know, you make sacrifices. That's family too.

At some point my dad told me, "If you go drinking some night, eat a cheeseburger before you get sloppy drunk. That way it will soak up the alcohol and you won't make a fucking idiot of yourself." That's a bit of his lasting guidance.

I never asked about personal stuff, maybe because of his silent nature, maybe because I was a kid, and what do you know when you're a kid? There's so much I don't know about him, and I regret that. I wish I had spent more time with the guy, but he could be distant, and he was intimidating. It wasn't just his size. It was the beard, the dark glasses, his tendency to be silent when angry. Sometimes I couldn't read his mood, and I think that scared me because I wasn't old enough or brave enough to understand.

Like all fathers, my dad had his faults, but *unlike* all fathers, he was there for his kids. He gave us life and did his best to raise us right. He wanted us to be good men, to hold the door for any lady, to say "sir" and "ma'am"—and to put up with zero shit.

He also encouraged us in our music. He turned me on to the Who, still my all-time favorite band. My friends were sneaking Van Halen and Kiss records into their dens when Mom and Dad were asleep, but my old man *played* them for me. As a disc jockey, he knew really good music. He wasn't a musician, but he had an ear for bullshit. That was his term. It was his job to be persnickety about music, and he imparted that to us.

Neither Zach nor I would have gone far without his encouragement. He bought us our first instruments, and we've been playing ever since. He never got to see our success, but I like to think nothing has escaped his sight. As long as it was on his left side.

That's a joke my dad would appreciate.

When my brother and I began taekwondo as kids, my dad took a few classes with us. He had a genuine interest in martial arts, but I think the strenuous activity was too much for him. He was in his late thirties then and not in the best physical condition. I remember him attempting to kick and punch. It didn't look good, and I felt awful for him. He lacked the flexibility, and I think the entire process was humiliating for him. He didn't want to embarrass us any further, so he quit. Here was something the man wanted to do, and he gave it up so his sons would not face ridicule.

He was forty-four when he received his cancer diagnosis. The disease didn't spring out of nowhere. It came from a lifetime of rough living, bad food, too much drink, and too much stress. We watched him go from 250 pounds to 125 in three months. The man became a skeleton.

His decline was quick until the last month. Then it seemed death was dawdling with the man. He had only enough strength to sit on the couch and watch the days pass.

In the movie version of this scene, you would see my dad there in front of the TV. The rest of us would be moving at four times normal speed, buzzing around him like flies around a dying husk.

We stayed in motion. He stayed put, watching and withering. Morning. Night. Another day gone. Stopping would mean considering what was about to happen. We'd have the rest of our lives for that.

My mom had always relied on my father for pretty much everything. They were married when she was nineteen. She was a kid, still living with her parents. My dad was the backbone of the relationship. In the final months of his life, that all changed. He had to depend on my mom for food, showers, and help to the bathroom. She had to be there and smile through it all so we couldn't see her pain. You never know what you're capable of until the circumstances demand action.

The Blairs were never a spiritual sort, but I did try praying once. I closed my eyes and said, "God, if you're there, please save my dad." He died a few months later. I was a nineteen-year-old idiot. Who can say how life would be different if he had lived?

When you're talking about life and death, maybe taekwondo doesn't sound like such a big deal. To me, it feels like everything. This whole endeavor is about tearing down the barriers that keep you from your dreams. Poverty? Physical limitations? Age? Fuck it. There has to be a way.

As I've made progress in taekwondo, I have felt this new connection with my old man. It's as though he's able to live this with me all these years later. I know that sounds weird, but it's what I feel.

And so, taekwondo is not about punching and kicking—not anymore. It's in the way I understand the world and myself. It's not a band situation and not a team effort. I do have the grandmaster, and my classmates, but ultimately, I do this or I don't. And if I don't, I have no one else to blame.

I walked away from the martial arts as a kid, and that's bothered me ever since. But more than anything, I'm doing this for my dad—because he could not. This is my second crack at taekwondo, and I have to get it right.

Man. I'm forty-fucking-three.

MARTIAL SPIRIT

Y OU ARE training, sweating your ass off. The visiting Koreans have honored you with an authentic workout. This is how they do it back home. I won't keep you in suspense: it's hard. Cardio drills, double kicks, laps, and high steppers. Stretches that would have made Plastic Man say, "I don't think so."

They pushed. Some purged. You hung in.

No one held back in sparring because there was nothing left to hold. You poured yourself onto the mat. You're dehydrated and exhausted, your breath slow and deliberate. That's all you're good for now, just breathing. You catch a glance from a classmate and share a smile of equal parts agony and relief.

You guys survived. Was that a spiritual experience? If so, was it somehow more spiritual than a good game of tennis?

For the rest of the day, you feel depleted but also fulfilled. A cold drink tastes better. A good meal is more satisfying. Is this what spirituality in the martial arts is all about? You weren't raising your hands and hollering for Jesus, but you still had an exorcism of sorts. Your mind is balanced, your heart at peace.

At home you may read a few pages from the *Dao Teh Ching* or a book on meditation. Then sleep will find you because you can't stay awake any longer. Is that spirituality? Is it just giving your all and being too exhausted to cause trouble?

I've heard a lot of talk about martial arts as a spiritual pursuit. Maybe it's because, for Westerners at least, training takes place in unfamiliar settings. You wear special clothes, bow a lot, and speak in tongues. The school acknowledges symbolic colors and insignias. Your classmates discuss lineage and venerate your forebears. You hear parables and think about life and death. Aside from all that shouting and breaking, the dojang is a quiet, reflective place. Some even have shrines.

You hear about the Dao, the path, the way. What is that? Your classmate has watched *Enter the Dragon* fifty times. He always recites that speech about filling the cup with the moon—or whatever. He wears a headband with an image of the rising sun. Is that spirituality?

Not many people look to the bassist for spiritual guidance, which is probably for the best, but after this time and research in martial arts, I feel like I should say a little something. For most of my life, I've abstained from religion or anything that smelled like it. My parents were hippies, and true to their counterculture, they shunned any bureaucracy that put God up for auction. At one point they said we could go to church on Sunday if we wanted. It was up to Zach and me. We chose cereal and cartoons instead. Hellfire and brimstone or Frosted Flakes and *G.I. Joe*? God, let me think about it.

I don't know my parents' beliefs, and that fact alone says a lot about their spirituality. I do think they believed in a higher power, but ultimately, Pat and Don just wanted us to be good, honest people. That was all the religion we needed. To them, being good was not about standing, sitting, and reciting, and it sure as hell wasn't about paying tithes. It was what you did, not what you said you would do.

My religious experiences include listening to Mozart's *Requiem*, playing in front of a huge crowd, and kissing my wife for the first time. I used to consider myself an atheist; now I'd say I am agnostic. God may be unknowable, but I remain open to the possibility.

I've always wondered what prayer has to do with nunchaku. Why is it that one person can see a martial art as a path to enlightenment and the way to know God while another can see that same art with no spiritual connotations?

Well, we can say the same about music. Johann Sebastian Bach said every note he played was for God. Listen to his music, and you can understand that. KISS just played to get chicks and rake in the money. Listen to their music, and you can understand that. Ultimately, these arts are in the hands of individuals—and their individual motivations, desires, and merchandise stands.

Buddhist monks trained in martial arts, so they saw the spiritual connotations. Samurais and ninjas saw them too, but for a different reason: they were preparing to battle for life and death. Those circumstances have turned a lot of people into believers.

I am a bassist, not a samurai or a theologian. If I found a spiritual awakening in taekwondo, that would be great—but I'm also sure if I don't get matters of the spirit, I can still get martial arts. For me, they are physical and intellectual pursuits. It's important to find your fighting spirit, but a religious quest should not get in the way of anyone's training. A religious quest is a different undertaking altogether.

Someone may tell me I'm missing the point, but I can say only what I know based on my experience. I remain open to a spiritual aspect of martial arts, but it's not my focus now. Maybe one day

I'll look back on this and say, "Man, I was unenlightened back then." Until that time, I will work from the concept I understand best: a martial art, at its core, is a way to train and focus—and keep from getting your ass kicked.

REFLECTIONS BEFORE
THE BIG TEST

MY BLACK-BELT test is a week and a half away. I hesitate to write about this before showtime, not because I'm superstitious but because that belt is not mine yet, and this is no time for an acceptance speech. I'm nervous, but I know the material. I should do all right, but there's still the actual execution.

If you commit to martial arts as a way of life, a test is just another day in the dojang. But the reality is that might be the day I see a childhood dream become reality—and at forty-three years of age. There's nothing mundane about that.

A lot has happened.

It's nearly December, and I've worked out every day since my last test. That was May. I used to take Sundays off, but I decided I needed all the repetitions I could get—and anyway, days off make me feel like a lazy turd. All that training has taken a toll on my body. The knees are shot. My left heel still hurts. My back aches on the left side, then the right. The pain moves around, but it always turns up somewhere.

But are we having fun? Well, taking a walk with the wife is fun. Playing *Halo* is fun. Taekwondo is something different. I still love getting up, putting on my dobok, and working out; it is, however, more of an obsession than a pastime.

Lately, I've been thinking about a different aspect of this taekwondo adventure. Pretty much every martial arts story ever written features the relationship between student and master. Kwai Chang Caine had Master Po. Daniel-san had Mr. Miyagi. The Bride had Bill.

Need more?

Shang-Chi had Fu Manchu. Iron Fist had Lei Kung the Thunderer. The Ninja Turtles had Splinter. Kung Fu Panda had Shifu.

Bruce Lee had Ip Man, Jackie Chan had Yu Jim Yuen, and Chuck Norris had Jesus.

When I started at the local WTF affiliate, I figured the grandmaster would be something like my ninja master. He'd correct my mistakes; yell at me when I needed it; and utter deep, awesome, mysterious truths for me to ponder. It didn't really work out that way. Maybe that happens only in movies.

He has instructed me, and I am grateful, but I've actually gained the most insight from my fellow students. Eric has taught me a lot. The grandmaster's son, Joe, has too. Those guys sharpened my strikes, blocks, and sparring. They watched me and set me straight. I studied their technique and tried to pick up on their strengths. I practiced every taegeuk a hundred times before showing the grandmaster for feedback. That was good. But I never had a "Snatch the pebble from my hand" moment with anyone.

The grandmaster traveled for work, and so did I. We had a professional relationship. It's been fine. But as I look back on all the stories in this book, I see that "Wax on, wax off" is missing. I never said, "Oh, that's it, Grandmaster. I get it now. Satori."

I'm not complaining about this, and I'm not blaming anyone. I'm just thinking.

I probably shouldn't think. I should just *be* and focus on the task at hand. I have to dig deep and be at my best to earn my black belt.

BLACK-BELT TEST

A T THE local WTF affiliate, the test for black belt typically comes in two different sessions. You take the first half, and six months later you take the second. This evening I went to the dojang to take part one. I stood in front of the grandmaster, and he introduced me to the packed room.

"We usually test students for their black in two parts," he said, "but Donivan will be taking both tests this evening."

I'm sure I made that face a baby makes when he craps his pants.

I don't know why the grandmaster made this decision, but I do know I was nervous enough already. After that, I felt like a jittery mess of adrenaline and puke. Shelley was there, and I had the support of my friends at the dojang, but support would get me only so far. I was the one taking the test. It was mine to pass or fail. I told myself I knew the material forward and backward, and I'd been preparing for this night for three years. I had to pull it together.

Before it was over I would need to perform nine forms, spar with two black belts at once, and break boards with five different kicks. Then the grandmaster would ask me to share my philosophy of taekwondo. If I made it through all that, I'd find out whether I passed. I might just head home that night a black belt.

To start I had to perform all eight taegeuk: Il Jang, Ee Jang, Sam Jang, Sa Jang, Oh Jang, Yuk Jang, Chil Jang, and Pal Jang. Then I performed the black-belt form, Koryo. I did them well enough. I was sweating and breathing so hard that if you added a wah pedal, you would have heard the sounds of seventies German porn.

There's an image you won't forget anytime soon.

We moved on to sparring. For the black-belt test you have to take on multiple opponents. I sparred with Sam and Lee at the same time. I felt like I was seconds away from a skinhead attack worthy of *American History X*, but I held my own.

One of my worst nightmares is not being able to break my boards. It happens to someone during every test. All you want to do is break them on your first shot, make the grandmaster smile, and be on your way so some other poor sap can have his turn in the crosshairs.

Another student, Gail, went before me. She was testing for her second-degree black belt, and she needed to break two boards at once with an axe kick. For the axe, you swing your leg up overhead and then drop it like the executioner's blade at the guillotine. The striking surface is the back of the heel. This girl could not get through those boards. After several attempts she left the room, sobbing. I felt horrible for her. I wished I could help, but what the hell could I do?

She finally composed herself, came back in the room, and smashed the hell out of the boards. Everyone yelled like it was a *Rocky* movie.

Then it was my turn. I took a few deep breaths to focus and slow my heart rate. We began with the jumping front. The last time I had attempted to break with that kick was during my red-belt test. It took me several tries then, so it was the kick I feared most—and because I feared it, something awful happened, something I hoped would never happen during my black-belt test: I got a visit from Coach and Ivan.

Ivan: I want to go home. Is this going to hurt? Let's go eat pizza.
Coach: Yes, this is going to hurt. Period. But it will hurt more if you don't do it. Now jump.

I jumped and threw a kick. The board shattered. The crowd cheered. One down, four to go. Next? The tornado.

Coach: Let's go, Sally. As soon as you break that board, you can go back to fruit booting.
Ivan: I'm not a fruit booter.
Coach: Well, you kick like one. Break!

Smash. Easy. More cheers. Two down. Next was the back kick.

Ivan: How do I—?
Coach: Back, like a donkey. Kick it, jackass.

Splinters. Woot, woot. The crowd was becoming more raucous as we went. On to the flying side kick.

Ivan: This will hurt my foot.
Coach: I'll fucking hurt your foot! Break!

Smash. Hong Kong Phooey would have been proud. Four up, four down.

The last kick was the spinning hook. I usually do it with my right foot, but the previous week, during my practice test, I was successful with my left. I thought I'd try that again.

Now, I have seen a bunch of black-belt tests, but I've never seen anyone break every board on the first try. I couldn't help but think I might be the first. My ego was getting out ahead of my foot.

Ivan: I'm gonna have such a cheeseburger after this.
Coach: Whatever you do, don't let this kick get into your head.

I spun and kicked. And my foot clunked off the board. No break. The crowd made a disappointed "Ahhh."

Ivan: I'm a failure.
Coach: It's OK. It happens to every guy. Try some Viagra.
   Then break that fucking board.

I spun again, kicked, and the board exploded. Coach and Ivan vanished in a puff of smoke. The crowd yelled and clapped. It's not every day you get to see a middle-aged man kill an entire forest with his bare feet. Pine trees will think twice before messing with me again.

Once we had littered the mat with splinters, the action was over, and we had to share what the grandmaster calls our master philosophies. These are our reflections on what we've learned since beginning taekwondo and how it has affected us. I said something like this:

My master philosophy is that taekwondo, while a martial art that can teach you how to defend yourself, is more than that. It's a way of life, and it has become so for me since I began training with the grandmaster. Taekwondo has taught me to exhibit control in areas I was not always good at. It's also shown me there are other things I can do with my life. It just takes hard work.

   We learn self-defense in taekwondo, but knowing kicks and punches is not what keeps us protected. It's the values and the self-control that allow us to live life and be better people.

We are lucky to be educated in a system with centuries of history. The first people to learn taekwondo had to show they were worthy of such knowledge by being good and honest, able to show kindness and restraint. I don't take this responsibility lightly, and neither do my fellow classmates. You have to be earnest in your pursuit of taekwondo and show you are here for the right reasons. The first time I stepped into the grandmaster's school, I knew I was at the right place for the right reasons.

I've been building to this test for the past three years of my life, and the fact that the grandmaster thinks I belong here is all I need, whether I pass or not.

After we all spoke, the grandmaster instructed us to remove our belts and stand before him. I had trained three years for that moment, but I'd waited over thirty years for it. The grandmaster tied my black belt around my waist—and then he hugged me. I could not believe it. He knows how hard I've trained and worked, but the man is not a hugger. For him to exhibit that much emotion meant a lot to me.

My classmates congratulated me with hugs and handshakes. It was over. I had made it.

The day had been so crazy and stressful that I didn't know how to feel. I was happy, of course, and relieved that I passed—and it was a vomit-free test, which was a bonus. But it finally hit me that I was really, really tired. I just wanted to sleep. In the morning I would figure out if my toes were broken. Shelley and I headed home.

I sent a message to my brother to share the good news. Thirty years later, I am a black belt. He wrote this: "Holy shit! I'm so proud of you! About fucking time!"

I went into the living room to show Shelley my latest contusion trophy. She spotted it before I could say anything. "Oh my God," She said. "Your foot!"

I have a big misshapen knot on my left toe. It's a weird gnarl, purple and black, the size of a quarter. I should be admiring my hard-earned black belt, but now that the day is over and I'm winding down, I'm sitting here looking at this tangible representation of Wolff's law.

Wolff's law tells us that changes in bone function cause changes in bone structure—that is, for the most part, the body adapts to the demands we make on it. We ask more, and the body does more to accommodate. Of course, the body also reserves the right to say fuck no. Those are the memorable moments when something tears or snaps or splits in half. Good fun.

Muay Thai kickboxers strike trees with their shins. That way, when they kick the living shit out of you, it destroys your bones, not theirs. Karate guys beat on makiwara, wooden boards with minimal padding. The methods vary, but the objective is the same.

Wolff's law explains why my foot doesn't hurt after two and a half years of breaking boards, but it must also have a psychological equivalent. We adapt to the loads we place upon our minds. Again, there are exceptions, but for the most part, we're stronger because of our hardships.

The tough guys and blowhards like to say, "What doesn't kill me makes me stronger." That's an oversimplification, and it's stupid when you think about it. What doesn't kill you might leave you a bleeding stump—definitely not stronger. Wolff's law is real and far more useful.

Enough of that. I can't believe I made it. I have a black belt. No, I *am* a black belt. I'm in the secret club, and I've passed the shadowy initiation. I worked hard, believed in myself, and accomplished something that normal people don't do.

Tonight I will go to sleep content. Tonight I will rest.

FEAR

THROUGHOUT THIS entire book I've preached perseverance, drive, giving it your all, and other inspiring awesomeness. I've gone into detail about getting hurt and about the times I got through training while gritting my teeth through the pain. At forty-three I earned my black belt—not as hard as becoming a Navy SEAL but not easy either.

Then something changed. Soon after my test for black, it hit me: I'm scared.

Now I have to talk myself into going to the dojang. When I get there, I have to take a few deep breaths before I go in. Why the hesitation? What's the worst that could happen? Well, I could get hurt. What if I break a bone or tear a ligament? What if I do worse?

There are certain rules in martial arts. Those rules vary by style—knife hands only, no weapons allowed, no Three Stooges finger pokes—but one rule that is universal in martial arts is this: you will get hurt. A lot.

If you attend a martial school where people aren't limping, constantly saying ow, and holding their sides because of bruised ribs, then leave. There's nothing for you to learn there.

When I first returned to taekwondo, I went to class as much as possible, feeling invincible. I was Wolverine, adamantium in my bones, and nothing could hurt me. Three years later, I accomplished my goal of becoming a black belt. But I did get hurt along the way: a bruised bone, hip pain, heel pain, a torn meniscus, and broken toes. Those injuries have stayed with me. Now I am reluctant and fearful. I'm not positive that this has to do with age, but it could. I find myself doubting my plans and less apt to take chances.

It's just a phase, I hope, and another situation to get through. Men have forever been assessing problems with themselves and pushing forward. I mean, Viagra? The only solution I see is to meet this head-on and continue to push. I'm a hardheaded Texan. That's what we do.

When I earned my yellow belt, I said a long-term goal was to kill the self-doubt. I have become a better martial artist since then. That much is clear. But I don't feel much more confident about any of this. I worry I'm not good enough and I'll get found out. "Ha! You should have stuck to playing bass. Rock star!"

There's a reason jockeys put blinders on horses. They only want them to see what's ahead and follow that path. No wandering off course, no deviation allowed. The horse keeps running no matter what, driven on by training and the cracking whip. Phantoms, snakes, and zombies could crawl to the edge of the track, but no worry. The goal is ahead. That is all.

I've had blinders on for most of my life. At fifteen I planned my career as a musician. I've had twists and turns, but I never strayed from that course. At forty I planned my new life as a martial artist. I kept running and carrying the load.

But what happens when the horse hits the finish line? The blinders come off. He doesn't know where to go. He's skittish, afraid.

As a kid I was the one who gave no thought before heading into danger. I would jump off of the tree house my grandfather had built for us. Nothing to worry about. I didn't know how to play bass, but I did it. I traveled the world without a second thought. I got married at twenty-two and never looked back. Faith and confidence in myself got me through.

Now I'm frightened. What's worse, I'm frightened *because* I'm scared. Am I the only guy who worries about this stuff? My fear stems not just from getting hurt, but getting hurt and being unable to continue. That would be death. And I'll be goddamned if I'm going to let death win.

NEW YEAR'S RESOLUTIONS

N EW YEAR'S Day. Another year gone, another one ahead. In December I fulfilled one of my lifelong goals. That felt amazing, no doubt about it, but the glow has worn off, and I'm no longer impressed with myself. All I can think is, "OK, I'm a black belt. Now what?" I need a new challenge.

The other day, the grandmaster told us he wanted to know our goals for the New Year. He said to keep them simple and attainable. "You and you only are responsible now for your progression in taekwondo," he added.

I know he's right. You get to the point where you no longer need training wheels, but you never stop falling down. You wobble and weave, and sometimes you end up on your ass. You just keep getting up. That's the mark of a good martial artist—and the measure of success in any endeavor.

But here's a confession: when the grandmaster asked for our goals, all I could think of was how I want to begin studying a different martial art. I want to go to a different school, train with other people, and take on a new challenge.

One reason, as I've mentioned, is that the grandmaster isn't around a whole lot. I wanted to get instruction from him, not some teenagers. That's frustrating. But I can't pin my restlessness on the grandmaster.

The main reason I think of moving on is a practical one, and I get a reminder of it every morning when I wake up. I drove my body into the concrete to reach black belt. As far as conditioning goes, I'm in the best shape of my life, but that's come at a real price. My bruises, tears, pulls, hyperextensions, and breaks are too many to list now. A black belt should be confident, right? I feel like all that's left of me is pulp and cinders.

It doesn't help that I evaluate my abilities against those of my classmates, who are younger and more athletic—and who recover faster from injury. I don't want anyone to say, "He's good . . . for a guy his age." Being good in my age category is not a barometer I'm content with. I guess I can't obsess about that too much because I would find students of all ages wherever I trained. I just know I don't want to become fat Elvis.

I've met a lot of people who puff up their chests and profess undying loyalty to taekwondo. It is the best, they say, the only real martial art. That's when I most need to talk with people interested in something more than dressing up in pajamas and smashing pine boards. The taekwondo-or-nothing mentality is shortsighted, and, really, it's stupid. It's like saying rock and roll is the only music that matters. Or saying, "I'm a Baptist, so Catholics are stupid—and Buddhists might as well be from another planet."

Right. Well, your loss.

Training in taekwondo has been awesome, but I don't feel that brand loyalty. I'm interested in all kinds of martial arts.

By the time I was a green belt, I'd seen several people reach black belt only to leave the school. I felt disgusted with them. Why do all that work and then walk away? Do you think you have nothing else to learn? Well, now I get it. I've been a devoted student of this art, and the art has done wonders for my life. But at this point the question is not whether taekwondo is right for me; the question is whether I'm right for taekwondo. If I can't perform at my highest level and give this 100 percent, I don't belong anymore.

Maybe I just need to meditate. That is one of my New Year's goals, actually. I've devoured my fair share of books on Buddhism, but always too fast, I think. They all say meditation is the great equalizer.

Don't like who you are? Meditate.

Need guidance on what to do and how to do it? Meditate.

Want to learn to fix a car? Go to mechanic school. Then meditate so you can be a better mechanic.

Whatever I resolve to do this year, meditation must come first. If it's the only thing I get right, it will be worthwhile. I think it's going to be a much-needed salve for my OCD.

So what next?

Should I quit taekwondo? Could I start over somewhere else? What about karate? How about Brazilian jiu-jitsu? It has never appealed to me, but that might be a good reason to try. Because I never thought I would. I don't know. I just feel if I stay in taekwondo, the chase is over. I don't see any real goals anymore, and I worry about a descent into complacency. What if I miss something better because I stayed with something familiar?

Obviously, whatever I do has to be the real thing. I've seen schools that advertise how to get your black belt in one year through the internet or correspondence. One of these is my friend's place in Amarillo. Nice guy, but come on. You can study Wing Chun gongfu online, and in twelve months you can have a black sash—along with a complimentary set of steak knives.

I'm at a split in the road. I'm looking both ways, and I'm not sure of the direction. It's normal to feel confused in the middle of a huge undertaking—college, for example, or a career, or trying to understand the Republican convention. I just know I don't want to reach fifty and think I wasted my last good physical years on the wrong style.

As I just wrote that line, my stomach dropped, like I was betraying my wife or something. What would I be betraying? Taekwondo? The grandmaster? Both have given me more than I can return. How do you return it anyway? Teach the next generation, I guess.

I could commit the rest of my training life to my familiar art, or I could push on and pursue another endeavor. What should I do? There's no quiet in my head today. I wish fat Elvis would leave me alone.

SO LONG

I HAVE left the dojang. I didn't make an announcement. I didn't have a falling-out with the grandmaster, the way some students do. I just left, and I'm not going back. This is not what I intended—not when I began my training and definitely not when I began this book.

I hoped the narrative would stay neat and orderly. I'd tell some stories about martial arts and rock and roll, and I'd crack some jokes. I'd learn taekwondo, push myself, and get beat up. Of course I hoped to become a black belt. Of course. Now that I am one, it's a little embarrassing to write that, but what can you do? I'm pretty sure anyone who is not a black belt wants to be one.

From a distance, it all seemed straightforward. Up close, it became more complicated. It turns out there's more to life in the dojang. You work hard, which is satisfying, but the place can also be political, insular, and stifling. You wear uniforms, but you are not the same. You have different needs and competing interests.

In working through all of this, I've spent a lot of time considering the role of the instructor. Who is a teacher, and what does he or she do? I've heard that those who can, do. Those who can't, teach. That's bullshit.

Who is born with the ability to light the stage on fire? Even Mozart had a teacher. It was his father. Before we met Amadeus, that kid was Joannes Chrysostomus, and he didn't know a G clef from an A# until Leopold showed him.

What would have become of the Beatles without George Martin as their producer?

Bruce Lee would have stayed a rowdy kid getting into turf wars if Ip Man had not shown him a different path.

Freddie Roach never reached a boxing title in his professional career. He got out, took his knowledge with him, and went on to train Oscar De La Hoya, Mike Tyson, and Manny Pacquiao. You've heard of them right?

Name a star, a hero, or a champion, and I guarantee there's a great teacher standing in the shadows. That teacher gives all to his students, becomes part of a long lineage, and lives on forever because of it.

In the beginning at least, the teacher-student relationship is simple: the one who knows leads the one who wants to know. When you feel you've found the right teacher, you think, "This is the place. I will follow my master until he dies or I do." And as martial arts movie protocol dictates, when he does die, you will walk out in the rain—it will certainly be raining that day—get on your knees, look to the sky, and scream, "Master!" Subtitles are optional.

Note: Make sure your teacher has actually passed. If he's just sleeping off a bender and you go through with the whole screaming thing, you're just going to feel silly.

Eventually the student becomes the master and leaves. Or the student thinks he's the master, leaves anyway, and charges more money for a watered-down version of what his teacher knew.

I've met some good teachers. If I encountered a bad one, I had the good fortune to suss him out before it was too late. Let's not talk about those four months of martial tutelage under the child-porn distributor. That would be a low blow at a time like this.

Most of us become a mishmash of what we pick up from several people in our lives. I learned how to play bass from two guys, Rob Tate and Tony Streetman. Rob would go over to my house and show me Iron Maiden songs. He was my first musical mentor. He was self-taught and one of those people who just instinctively knew how to play bass. He encouraged me to learn for myself.

Streetman was different. He was a multi-instrumentalist and adept at everything. Plus he was a genius. And rich. And girls loved him. I have no idea why the guy hung out with me. I lowered his property value.

When Maiden and Sabbath riffs weren't doing it anymore, I needed fresh input. Streetman came in, turned me on to modes and scales, and awakened my desire to learn music theory. I took college classes to fill in the details. Then I took up punk rock and threw away everything I'd learned.

When my old band Hagfish went into the studio to make the record . . . *Rocks Your Lame Ass*, our producers were Bill Stevenson and Stephen Egerton. Stevenson was the drummer of Black Flag; Egerton played guitar in Decendents. We were in our twenties and thrilled to be in a real studio. We thought it would be fun. It wasn't. Stevenson and Egerton ran the sessions like drill sergeants. They did all they could to haze us. They belittled us, baited us, and made our lives miserable at every opportunity.

The first time our singer George sang for them, he went into the vocal booth and performed one of the new songs. When he finished, all was quiet. He said into the mic, "How was that, guys?"

Stevenson got on the talkback and said, "That was probably the shittiest singing I've ever heard."

These guys were our heroes, and they were beating the piss out of us. I had to track all of my bass lines in one day, and it was in the control room, sitting between the two of them. I should have worn an army helmet.

They gave us homework. They made us slow down and practice to a click, even George, even in rehearsal. They hammered us on our phrasing. Upstrokes, downstrokes . . . what are you guys doing here? Stevenson heard our stock backing vocals and sent us to the record store for a copy of the Beach Boys' *Pet Sounds*.

Could those two be mean? Yes. Were they sadistic? Definitely. But did we learn? Oh man, did we. They built us up by tearing us down. They taught me about music, but in a bigger sense, they taught me the importance of having good teachers, and with those two I had the best.

When Shelley and I moved to Amarillo, I befriended Barry, and that set me on the martial course I am still traveling. I visited a lot of other schools and teachers over the years. Each time, I observed, evaluated, and asked myself the same question: "Is this the guy?" I had watched way too many kung fu flicks and gotten sucked into the master-teacher mythology. I was ready to hand over my life to an instructor, if only I found the right one. It wasn't until I went to the local WTF affiliate that I found solace and quit looking. I was content and stable, and every day I had discoveries and breakthroughs. If I spent four hours doing only kicks—slow, focused, methodical kicks—then I considered that time a success. I learned something and got just a little better. That was the objective.

Toward the end I became disenchanted with the grandmaster's school. I think that's become clear in my writing of late. I resented that he barred me from the taekwondo tournament, but I could live with that.

It hurt more when my friends Conner and Spencer left the school. They were older black belts, and I looked up to them. At the time I couldn't understand it. Why would they leave after all that hard work? I told myself I would never do that. Looking back,

I get it. They walked out, as I've said, mainly because the grand-master was not around enough, and they were not thrilled about taking instruction from teenagers. I feel the same. I'm spending a lot of time and money to study with the grandmaster. The teenage black belts are really good, but if they opened their own school, I wouldn't go study with them. I'd go with the older Korean guy who had been everywhere and done everything.

Another difficulty arose when Team Blair had some financial trouble. My wife had lost her job, and the next day I got hit with a $9,000 tax bill. I freaked. I began thinking of ways to cut losses and shrink our debts. We cut our cable TV and stopped going out to eat, and I made the decision to drop my taekwondo classes. The Toadies had elected to take time off, and it wasn't like I was earning big money with my day job. Training is important to me, make no mistake, but my priority was getting us out of financial trouble. The dojang would still be there.

On January 1 I paid for an entire year of lessons with the grand-master. It seemed safe enough at the time. Then our finances went down the crapper. I had a meeting with the grandmaster and told him what Shelley and I were up against. I wondered if perhaps I could get a refund on my tuition. There was no way I could look my wife in the eye and say, "I know that we owe nine grand, you're not working, and I make ten bucks an hour, but I gotta pay my taekwondo bill. Priorities, baby."

The grandmaster listened to my problem but said the school does not give refunds. He apologized about the situation and offered me a loan. There was no way I could accept that. Accruing new debt to pay off old debt never solves anything. I appreciated his sincerity in wanting to help, but if he could have made an exception to his policy and given me a refund, it would have meant so much. At that moment, I needed to pay bills, not learn a Z kick.

I don't mean this as an indictment. It's just a summary of what got me here. Whenever you want to break up with someone, you start watching for reasons to cut out. Once you find what you need, bam—there's your answer. My reasons for staying with the grand-master were dwindling; my justification for leaving was only getting stronger.

There's also the matter of this old body. Taekwondo is built on kicking techniques, and they are hard to do with forty-three-year-old knees and hips. I keep trying, but I am dealing with persistent pain, and it isn't getting any better. What happens when I hit fifty? I've seen too many "masters" who can't get their legs up high enough because of a hip surgery or some nagging injury, and I'm sure not going to be the elder black belt telling people what to do if I can't do it. Better to find something a guy my age can carry out.

What really surprised me was the disenchantment I felt after I got my black belt. I put in all that work, all those crazy hours, and I endured the pain to make my childhood dream come true. And that dream did come true. Then the balloon burst.

"What next?" I thought.

I assumed I would stay on, maybe even reach master one day. It gave me a long-term goal, which always keeps me centered. I stayed busy with training daily and teaching when called upon. When the grandmaster asked me to lead class, I took it seriously and gave it my best. Some of the other kids, because they were kids, would hem and haw. They weren't sure what to teach. If the grandmaster said, "Donivan, lead class," I had to come up with a plan on the spot and stick to it. I did that, and I did my best. But I could feel my enthusiasm fading.

The cranky old farts of the martial arts always bemoan the loss of tradition. They say we aren't dedicated the way they were. We don't work hard the way they did. We aren't loyal the way they were. They can't make a single pronouncement unless it begins with "nowadays"—as in, "Nowadays, students don't . . . ."

By leaving the grandmaster, I've become more evidence of their worldview. If they cared enough to read this book, they would walk away saying, "Blair approaches the dojang as a consumer. Sell him what he wants, or else he'll take his business to another shop."

Well, you know what?

Touché.

But I'd find that argument more compelling if we lived in an agrarian society in ancient China. There, if I were lucky, I'd have one teacher close enough to walk to. I'd beg him to take me as a student, and if he agreed, I'd be with him for life. I'd have to accept whatever lessons he gave me and remain ignorant of whatever he held back. He might be great. He might not. There would be no competition and thus no reason for him to get better. I wouldn't be able to find another teacher, and moving away from the family farm would not be an option.

I think—*nowadays*—in martial arts and pretty much every other endeavor, competition is good for everyone. Everyone.

Now I am certain about leaving, but arriving at this decision was hell. Taekwondo had kept me centered for years. If I stopped training, would I go nuts? I lost sleep agonizing over it. I paced and sweated it out. I imagined how a recovering addict feels, living with constant worry, the specter of relapse never far. I don't think I'm being melodramatic here. If I'm not giving my all, I go fucking mental.

I owe the grandmaster for getting me here, this version of me that's calmer and more focused. I will forever be indebted to him and his school for shaping me into the man I am today. The guy who walked into that first class is not the same guy who is walking out.

WE FIGHT ON

I HAVE this idea for a movie. It's about a guy who's in a popular band, but he's about to quit touring and go home to his girl for good. They've made plans for their new life and all the adventures they will have together. A few days before his final gig, he walks offstage and checks his text messages. He has dozens waiting for him.

The first one is from his sister. It says, "I'm so, so sorry. Call me if you need anything."

Something is wrong here.

The guy's girl has been killed in a car wreck. He's destroyed. He leaves the band, but when he gets home, he can't stand the silence. His girl is gone, and all the plans they made are lost.

What follows is a fast decline into drinking, drugs, and bankruptcy. I know it's melodramatic, like an episode of VH1's *Behind the Music*, but stay with me.

The guy ends up in a rundown apartment and eventually takes a crappy job at a convenience store. One night he leaves work and walks down the street. He stops in front of a kickboxing school. He's never been into martial arts, but he thinks, "What the hell? What have I got to lose?"

He gets himself straight, and he trains day and night because training is the only thing that makes him feel OK. He joins a tournament and wins. He gets more fights and more victories. The crowds get bigger, and the prizes get better.

Finally, he gets booked for a major bout. The purse is enough to get him out of debt. We're not talking about retirement here, but if he wins, he will have earned some measure of redemption from that darkest period of his life.

The big fight is difficult and bloody. Our hero and his opponent are an even match. They beat the crap out of each other. The final bell rings, and it goes to decision. The fighters spit out blood, wipe their faces, and join the referee in the center of the ring.

The announcer says, "Ladies and gentlemen," and goes through his patter. The crowd buzzes. The music swells. He gets to "And the winner is . . ."

And the screen goes black. The credits roll.

I know mainstream audiences would never tolerate that. They need winners and losers. This will have to be a short film that never makes it further than indie festivals. But I'm sure you see what I'm thinking here.

Who cares who won? If our protagonist loses the bout, do we change our feelings about him? Does it negate his story?

The spoils of victory are superficial and visible to all: houses, cars, bling . . . a '57 Les Paul Goldtop. But real success is personal. It's all about the story and the struggle, and that goes way down into our marrow.

The stories that inspire us don't have to end like a *Rocky* movie. We should measure victory by getting up, by never giving up.

That's what I like about this short film in my head. Maybe our hero wins and his metamorphosis is complete. Maybe he wins and discovers he doesn't feel redeemed at all, so he needs something else. Maybe he loses and ends up in a gutter. Or maybe he loses but it doesn't matter because he realizes the work he put in turned his life around. That's the bigger victory.

If success is relative, failure must be too. We're all afraid to fail, but falling short of a goal is not the worst thing that can happen to a person. My real fear is that I'll stop striving, that I'll drift toward stasis, apathy, and atrophy.

* * *

I came of age in the eighties. Madonna and the Boss ruled music on the radio and TV. If you didn't have an interesting look and a trendy sound, you wouldn't get a major-label deal—and if you didn't get a major-label deal, chances were good you'd be stuck in Sherman, Texas, or somewhere equally hopeless and shitty. You'd get hitched to the neighborhood bicycle, live out your clichés, and then you'd die.

That would have been me if I hadn't found punk rock.

When I was seventeen, I was hanging out with my friend Tony. He was already twenty-one, and he'd lived in Los Angeles for a year, a fact that made him far cooler than anyone I had ever met. LA, man. Holy shit. He got turned on to a ton of great bands when he was out there, so when he went back to Sherman, he took a killer record collection with him. If it hadn't been for Tony, I wouldn't know Fugazi from the Fugees.

One night some friends and I went to a house party. Tony and I were watching my classmates drink themselves into oblivion. For many of them, it was the beginning of a spiral into the whiskey dickdom from which they'd never recover. It all seemed so stupid to me, and I guess Tony could tell that by my expression.

"Do you ever get messed up?" he said.

"Hell no," I said.

"You and your brother don't do anything?" he asked. "Drugs? Beer even?"

"Nope."

At that moment we watched a guy I had grown up with puke and fall into it. He was with a gorgeous girl I had crushed on for a long time. She helped him up and gave him another beer.

What a fucking waste, I thought. If this is what you have to do to fit in, to be someone, then count me out. I never belonged anyway. Why try now?

"So you're straight edge then?" Tony said.

"What the hell is that?" I said. I thought it was some hippie shit, which is funny because it's pretty much the opposite of hippie shit.

"It means no drugs, no alcohol, and no promiscuous sex."

"Then yes, I'm straight edge," I said. I thought about it a moment. "Is the no-sex part optional?"

In the early eighties Ian MacKaye of Minor Threat wrote a song called "Straight Edge." It's forty-four seconds long. It's fast and aggressive, and MacKaye sings—shouts, really—that he has more to do with his life than get fucked up all the time. He doesn't point fingers or make accusations; he just takes a stand.

I had seen the trouble alcohol brought my mom and dad, and I was seeing what drugs were doing to some of my peers. So fuck it. I didn't need any of that.

That's the positive side of straight-edge culture: sobriety, clear judgment, self-determinism. There is a darker side. Straight-edge people can be snobbish, fanatical, and even militant. Some say you can't be straight edge if you have caffeine. Some say you can never take aspirin. I've had twenty-year-olds tell me I'm not edge because I eat meat.

At seventeen I had found a culture I actually identified with. My only potential problem was the rule against having sex. I knew I could abstain from drugs and alcohol because people offered them to me and I said no. As for sex, I didn't exactly have girls chasing me down. It was easy to say, "I don't wish to engage in such activities" when the reality was that females found me quite unscrewable. Maybe it was the unkempt hair, snaggle teeth, and awkwardness that kept me a virgin so long. Seventeen was late compared to a lot of kids. It sure as hell felt late to me then. I was a horny Texas teen who would have fucked a fruit basket if it had lipstick on.

Sherman didn't have a straight-edge scene per se. Zach and I had to visit Dallas for a glimpse of the punk world, and when we did, I discovered that most punkers looked at straight kids as dorks. Punkers are outcasts, and as a straight-edge kid I had joined the chess club of punk rock. Hot. I couldn't even *not* fit in right.

But we all had Black Flag's *My War*, so in one way or another everything was OK.

When I dove into punk music, my future came into focus. A kid from Sherman would never end up in A Flock of Seagulls or Duran Duran, but MacKaye and Greg Ginn of Black Flag showed me the way. It wasn't paved with gold, but at least it led out of north Texas.

Punk guys were not household names, but they made their own rules. They were their own bosses, and they created the music they wanted to make. Some ran their own record labels but not in a traditional sense—usually out of someone's living room. They didn't need radio, *Billboard* magazine, or MTV, and they sure as hell didn't need a focus group to tell them what was in their hearts.

Poison and Bon Jovi played the game, just as the rock stars du jour do now. Does "Livin' on a Prayer" give you the spastic energy of "Guilty of Being White"? It doesn't do it for me.

Even Metallica, the beacon of hope for every thirteen-year-old musician jamming in the garage, signed a deal with Elektra Records. Metallica, Maiden, and Priest said they did it for the kids. At some point I said bullshit. Those guys did it for themselves and for the company, and I was tired of feeling like a sucker. I heard Bad Religion and I swear on my father's grave that light split the clouds and blinded me. I heard X, Descendents, Bad Brains, Dag Nasty, Circle Jerks, and Gorilla Biscuits, and I was transformed.

My punk heroes weren't much older than I was. Most were in their early twenties, already living their dreams. They were doing exactly as they wanted and answering to no one. There was a positive message in all that awesome noise. These guys spoke against conformity, hypocrisy, and greed. They stood for the individual.

I could do this.

No record executive took interest in Black Flag, so what did they do? Started their own label and toured the world. Don't want to hear it? Here it is anyway. Your club doesn't want us? Awesome. We'll hire out the union hall and have the show without your approval.

That is punk rock, taking a no and turning it into a great big fuck you.

Let's hit fast forward on this DIY cassette.

My friend Aaron Bedard was the singer for Bane, a very influential straight-edge band. His nickname was Sticks back in the day because he was so freaking skinny. I was in Only Crime, and we went on tour with Bane for three weeks. People in the straight-edge scene can be very clannish, dressing alike, drawing a black X on the back of each hand, and listening to the exact same records. If you don't have everything Earth Crisis recorded, you're out.

Nearly every night Sticks would give his rap. He could be very positive and deliver uplifting speeches from the stage. As soon as he began speaking, the kids went from an unruly herd to a society of rapt attention. He'd start with how great it was to see so many people embracing the straight-edge lifestyle. The crowd would roar. Then he'd mention how proud he was that a lot of teens were straight edge. Another roar.

Then he'd say, "I think it's great you're doing this, but how about you figure out *who* you are before you decide *what* you are?"

Silence.

The kids had come for a religious experience. Even if they were tough and determined, they could be insecure too. They trusted

Aaron. They memorized his words and believed in his message. He was not supposed to do that to them—which was exactly why he did it.

I've seen a lot of zealots declare their fervor for straight living. They swear they will never drink or use drugs for the rest of their lives, and they may be only eighteen. A lot of them go to college a few months later, and then it's all over. They grow dreads and get baked listening to Bob Marley.

I'm not judging. *Exodus* is a great record. And anyway, it's none of my business. People have to make their own decisions. I've made mine, and I haven't always been proud of them.

I turned forty on tour with the Toadies. We played in Winnipeg that night, and after the show the guys insisted on buying me a shot of whiskey for every decade I had been alive. I looked at those four dark glasses. Eighty proof. I drank them down.

Just to be clear, this is not the band's fault. It's not Jack Daniel's either. No one held a gun to my head. This is all mine, and I'll own it. But it's also a reminder that you never outgrow peer pressure, even when you're forty fucking years old.

The next morning I woke up with a dim thrumming in my head. I'd be lying if I said I didn't think about my wife and my folks. I thought about my brother and our shared Irish Cherokee lineage. If anyone should stay away from alcohol, it's the Irish Cherokee kids.

Well, shit.

I had a cup of coffee and moved on.

*   *   *

For decades I dreamed of returning to taekwondo. I've done that, and it's been one of the most challenging and most rewarding experiences of my life. Writing a book isn't easy either.

Today if someone told me "I'd like to learn martial arts, but I'm afraid I'm too old now," here is what I'd say:

Put yourself in a class with physically gifted teenagers, and you'll be compelled to show you can hang. Don't prove that to anyone else. You only have to prove it to you. You will never face an opponent who is craftier, faster, or stronger than the one who exists in your mind.

That's not just a lesson from martial arts.

Training is tough. Getting older is tough too, but it's still better than the alternative. My dad died in his forty-fourth year, and at some point I realized I had lived longer than he did. It was as though I'd crossed into uncharted territory.

I'm not going anywhere. It will be a long, long time before I check out—at least I hope so. But now and then I catch a glimpse of my own mortality. I realize the days are passing and I'm not going to live forever. No one will. Except maybe Keith Richards.

We never know when we'll play our last song or throw our last kick. We don't know when we'll see our parents for the final time. We can't say how, when, or where the story will end. Like the musician turned kickboxer in my short film, we are in the fight of our lives until the screen goes black.

But also like that kickboxer, we fight on until that moment.

ACKNOWLEDGEMENTS

ANY CREATIVE endeavor should be a cleansing of sorts, kind of like a good colonic. In the process of writing this book, I discovered some things about myself I'm not proud of—and I listed them in detail for everyone to read. I've also found things I am proud of and never recognized until I sat down and wrote them out. I couldn't afford therapy, so I got into my jammies, kicked other people, and wrote about it.

I would like to thank everyone who played some part in this. Sorry if I kicked you.

My wife, Shelley, who believed in me so much and insisted I should start writing. This is for you. I just finished a book, but I still don't have the chops to convey my love for you.

Thanks to . . .

my brother, Zach, who is not only my sibling but my best friend on the planet. The only reason I got to travel the world was by hanging onto his coattails.

my mom, Patricia, who taught me how to cuss and made sure I used correct pronunciation while doing it. She also loved me no matter what I said or did, right or wrong.

my dad, Donald. I wouldn't know how or what to read if it had not been for him. My hope in life is that I have made him proud.

the staff at *Tae Kwon Do Times*, including former managing editor Michael Davis, who first published my writing.

David Ripianzi and T. G. LaFredo for their support, for not throwing my "manuscript" in the trash, and for giving me hope that I could do this. Axie Breen for the perfect cover. Doran Hunter for editing. Cecilia Alejandra Blair for the portrait.

my bandmates and crew, Mark Reznicek, Vaden Todd Lewis, and Clark Vogeler; Matt Lindquist, Dale Brock, and Tami Thomsen. This thank-you isn't as good as a basket of fruit, but it will have to do.

the grandmaster, for welcoming me into your school and making a martial artist out of me.

my instructors and training partners: Brandon Landelius (my partner in crime), Professor Chad Smith, and Professor Guilherme "Seco" Campos. Everyone at the local WTF affiliate and Guetho Texas BJJ.

.

About the Author

Donivan Blair plays bass in the rock band the Toadies. He holds a black belt in tae-kwondo and trains in a shed behind his house. He and his wife, Shelley, live in Amarillo, Texas.

(Photo by Cecilia Alejandra Blair)

BOOKS FROM YMAA

101 REFLECTIONS ON TAI CHI CHUAN
108 INSIGHTS INTO TAI CHI CHUAN
ADVANCING IN TAE KWON DO
ANALYSIS OF SHAOLIN CHIN NA 2ND ED
ANCIENT CHINESE WEAPONS
THE ART AND SCIENCE OF STAFF FIGHTING
ART OF HOJO UNDO
ARTHRITIS RELIEF, 3D ED.
BACK PAIN RELIEF, 2ND ED.
BAGUAZHANG, 2ND ED.
BRAIN FITNESS
CARDIO KICKBOXING ELITE
CHIN NA IN GROUND FIGHTING
CHINESE FAST WRESTLING
CHINESE FITNESS
CHINESE TUI NA MASSAGE
CHOJUN
COMPREHENSIVE APPLICATIONS OF SHAOLIN CHIN NA
CONFLICT COMMUNICATION
CROCODILE AND THE CRANE: A NOVEL
CUTTING SEASON: A XENON PEARL MARTIAL ARTS
    THRILLER
DEFENSIVE TACTICS
DESHI: A CONNOR BURKE MARTIAL ARTS THRILLER
DIRTY GROUND
DR. WU'S HEAD MASSAGE
DUKKHA HUNGRY GHOSTS
DUKKHA REVERB
DUKKHA, THE SUFFERING: AN EYE FOR AN EYE
DUKKHA UNLOADED
ENZAN: THE FAR MOUNTAIN, A CONNOR BURKE MARTIAL
    ARTS THRILLER
ESSENCE OF SHAOLIN WHITE CRANE
EXPLORING TAI CHI
FACING VIOLENCE
FIGHT BACK
FIGHT LIKE A PHYSICIST
THE FIGHTER'S BODY
FIGHTER'S FACT BOOK
FIGHTER'S FACT BOOK 2
FIGHTING THE PAIN RESISTANT ATTACKER
FIRST DEFENSE
FORCE DECISIONS: A CITIZENS GUIDE
FOX BORROWS THE TIGER'S AWE
INSIDE TAI CHI
KAGE: THE SHADOW, A CONNOR BURKE MARTIAL ARTS
    THRILLER
KATA AND THE TRANSMISSION OF KNOWLEDGE
KRAV MAGA PROFESSIONAL TACTICS
KRAV MAGA WEAPON DEFENSES
LITTLE BLACK BOOK OF VIOLENCE
LIUHEBAFA FIVE CHARACTER SECRETS
MARTIAL ARTS ATHLETE
MARTIAL ARTS INSTRUCTION
MARTIAL WAY AND ITS VIRTUES
MASK OF THE KING
MEDITATIONS ON VIOLENCE
MERIDIAN QIGONG EXERCISES
MIND/BODY FITNESS
THE MIND INSIDE TAI CHI
THE MIND INSIDE YANG STYLE TAI CHI CHUAN
MUGAI RYU
NATURAL HEALING WITH QIGONG
NORTHERN SHAOLIN SWORD, 2ND ED.
OKINAWA'S COMPLETE KARATE SYSTEM: ISSHIN RYU
POWER BODY
PRINCIPLES OF TRADITIONAL CHINESE MEDICINE
QIGONG FOR HEALTH & MARTIAL ARTS 2ND ED.
QIGONG FOR LIVING

QIGONG FOR TREATING COMMON AILMENTS
QIGONG MASSAGE
QIGONG MEDITATION: EMBRYONIC BREATHING
QIGONG MEDITATION: SMALL CIRCULATION
QIGONG, THE SECRET OF YOUTH: DA MO'S CLASSICS
QUIET TEACHER: A XENON PEARL MARTIAL ARTS THRILLER
RAVEN'S WARRIOR
REDEMPTION
ROOT OF CHINESE QIGONG, 2ND ED.
SCALING FORCE
SENSEI: A CONNOR BURKE MARTIAL ARTS THRILLER
SHIHAN TE: THE BUNKAI OF KATA
SHIN GI TAI: KARATE TRAINING FOR BODY, MIND, AND
    SPIRIT
SIMPLE CHINESE MEDICINE
SIMPLE QIGONG EXERCISES FOR HEALTH, 3RD ED.
SIMPLIFIED TAI CHI CHUAN, 2ND ED.
SIMPLIFIED TAI CHI FOR BEGINNERS
SOLO TRAINING
SOLO TRAINING 2
SUDDEN DAWN: THE EPIC JOURNEY OF BODHIDHARMA
SUMO FOR MIXED MARTIAL ARTS
SUNRISE TAI CHI
SUNSET TAI CHI
SURVIVING ARMED ASSAULTS
TAE KWON DO: THE KOREAN MARTIAL ART
TAEKWONDO BLACK BELT POOMSAE
TAEKWONDO: A PATH TO EXCELLENCE
TAEKWONDO: ANCIENT WISDOM FOR THE MODERN
    WARRIOR
TAEKWONDO: DEFENSES AGAINST WEAPONS
TAEKWONDO: SPIRIT AND PRACTICE
TAO OF BIOENERGETICS
TAI CHI BALL QIGONG: FOR HEALTH AND MARTIAL ARTS
TAI CHI BALL WORKOUT FOR BEGINNERS
TAI CHI BOOK
TAI CHI CHIN NA: THE SEIZING ART OF TAI CHI CHUAN,
    2ND ED.
TAI CHI CHUAN CLASSICAL YANG STYLE, 2ND ED.
TAI CHI CHUAN MARTIAL APPLICATIONS
TAI CHI CHUAN MARTIAL POWER, 3RD ED.
TAI CHI CONNECTIONS
TAI CHI DYNAMICS
TAI CHI FOR DEPRESSION
TAI CHI IN 10 WEEKS
TAI CHI QIGONG, 3RD ED.
TAI CHI SECRETS OF THE ANCIENT MASTERS
TAI CHI SECRETS OF THE WU & LI STYLES
TAI CHI SECRETS OF THE WU STYLE
TAI CHI SECRETS OF THE YANG STYLE
TAI CHI SWORD: CLASSICAL YANG STYLE, 2ND ED.
TAI CHI SWORD FOR BEGINNERS
TAI CHI WALKING
TAIJIQUAN THEORY OF DR. YANG, JWING-MING
TENGU: THE MOUNTAIN GOBLIN, A CONNOR BURKE
    MARTIAL ARTS THRILLER
TIMING IN THE FIGHTING ARTS
TRADITIONAL CHINESE HEALTH SECRETS
TRADITIONAL TAEKWONDO
TRAINING FOR SUDDEN VIOLENCE
WAY OF KATA
WAY OF KENDO AND KENJITSU
WAY OF SANCHIN KATA
WAY TO BLACK BELT
WESTERN HERBS FOR MARTIAL ARTISTS
WILD GOOSE QIGONG
WOMAN'S QIGONG GUIDE
XINGYIQUAN

DVDS FROM YMAA

more products available from . . .

YMAA Publication Center, Inc. 楊氏東方文化出版中心

1-800-669-8892 • info@ymaa.com • www.ymaa.com